Mountain Bike Training

For Marion

Achim Schmidt

Mountain Bike Training
For All Levels of Performance

Meyer & Meyer Sport

Original Title: Mountainbiketraining für Anfänger und Profis
Aachen: Meyer & Meyer 2012
Translated by: Heather Ross

British Library Cataloguing in Publication Data
A catalogue record for this book is available from the British Library

Mountain Bike Training
2nd revised edition 2014
Maidenhead: Meyer & Meyer Sport (UK) Ltd., 2014
ISBN: 978-1-78255-014-3

© 2014 by Meyer & Meyer Sport (UK) Ltd.
2nd revised edition 2014
Aachen, Auckland, Beirut, Budapest, Cairo, Cape Town, Dubai, Hägendorf,
Indianapolis, Maidenhead, Singapore, Sydney, Tehran, Wien
Member of the World
Sport Publishers' Association (WSPA)
Printed and bound by: B.O.S.S Druck und Medien GmbH
ISBN 978-1-78255-014-3
www.m-m-sports.com
E-Mail: info@m-m-sports.com

Contents

1   Introduction

1.1   How to Use This Book

This book is intended for active mountain bikers, whether they take part in races or just do the sport to keep fit, and also for coaches, exercise instructors and physios in competitive mountain biking.

Unlike the many existing mountain bike books that deal with technique or bike repair, this one focuses exclusively on the training for the various performance factors in mountain biking. Cycling technique has already been sufficiently covered in other books and is only addressed in passing in chapter 8, Technique Training, which details the training methods used for practicing the correct techniques.

For a better understanding of the specialized chapters, chapter 2, The Physiology and Anatomy of the Mountain Biker, is particularly recommended for those readers who lack a basic grounding in anatomy and physiology, although subsequent chapters can be understood without this knowledge. Just as important as the physiological and anatomical basics are the basics of training methodology, which are explained at the beginning of each section in chapter 3.

The aim of the book is to enable the reader, once he has studied it in detail, to draw up his own training plan.

The detailed table of contents allows the reader to quickly locate specific topics so that the book can also be used as a reference.

Training Plans

The training plans presented in different chapters are just suggestions, each category designed for an average cyclist. Goals, available training time and personal fitness levels obviously vary from person to person, so it is essential to adapt or correct the plans to suit your own needs. The plans are not intended for elite cyclists, but for the majority of average mountain bikers, whether they do the sport competitively, as a hobby or to keep fit.

As described in chapter 3, the difficulty of training planning and execution increases as performance levels improve. At an elite level, there is a fine line between over- and undertraining, and details can make the difference between peak form and loss of form and, therefore, between victory and defeat.

The beginner should realize that when starting an endurance sport, training progress may be very rapid, but after six to nine months, performance improvement slows down. Several years of planning and regular and consistent training are required just to reach a good regional level, if the rider doesn't already have an endurance background from another sport. This is true for all endurance sports, not just mountain biking.

It is even more difficult in road racing, which is mentioned when the training methods overlap. The races with a peloton lack the individual timing factor of a mountain bike race or a triathlon. Beginners must, as a rule, drop out of the race if they fall behind the peloton, but in mountain biking it is more or less every man for himself.

1.2 Developments in Mountain Biking

The Beginning

When in 1974 the first enthusiasts, notably Gary Fisher and Tom Ritchey, started riding down the mountains around Mount Tamalpais near San Francisco on old, classic cruisers, they had no idea of the boom that would follow with the invention of the mountain bike. A little later, these enthusiasts added gears to their bikes, thus creating the first genuinely off-road mountain bikes. Now they could not only ride down the mountains, but go back up again under their own steam. At the end of the 1970s, the first mountain bikes were produced in large quantities in sunny California. Almost immediately afterward, the first industrial production centers were moved to Southeast Asia, and thanks to greater quantities and lower prices, mountain bikes also took the European market by storm. The modern components giant Shimano also underwent a boom thanks to countless technical mountain bike innovations.

The first mountain bike races on Mount Tamalpais were downhills with a mass start, and cross-country and uphill races were soon added. In 1990, the sport of mountain biking was officially recognized by the world association, the UCI (Union Cycliste Internationale), and the first World Cup was launched in 1991. Prior to this, from 1987 to 1990, there had been three years of two competing World Championships organized by two associations.

In addition to the above-mentioned races, you can also enter dual slaloms and various trial, fun and stunt competitions as well as speed biking races, in which speed records are attempted.

The development of the mountain bike has not only had an impact on competition, but also on health, leisure and hobby activities. Cycling has experienced a boom that shows no sign of tailing off. In fact, the bicycle as transportation is even increasing in popularity due to environmental and traffic problems.

Cruisers were the forerunners of mountain bikes.

What is the special appeal of mountain biking?

Mountain biking's all-terrain suitability allows riders to find their own path off the beaten track. It appeals to the spirit of discovery in all of us. It is exciting to explore an area that you have previously only traveled through by car and find hidden areas of natural beauty. The slower speed of the mountain bike allows you to really get close to nature on small trails and paths away from the busy roads where you can explore and actively experience beautiful countryside.

As greater distances can be covered by bike than on foot, even remote places can be reached in a day. You can stop at any time to rest, look around and enjoy the view. On long rides, which may even push you to the limit of your performance, in the perfect and back-to-basics environment you may rediscover forgotten feelings such as hunger and thirst. The feeling of sinking exhausted onto your bed after a hard day's cycle is another undeniable highlight of a new attitude to life.

As well as all these rather obvious attractions, we can also add the thrill of a fast downhill ride and the feeling of gliding—similar to skiing—that the biker always rediscovers in the mountains. The difficulty of riding down a narrow trail against the resistance of gravity and centrifugal force, or using all one's strength and skill to negotiate a steep incline, are sensations that excite bikers and keep them coming back for more.

Stunts and Trial

Playing with gravity is particularly fascinating for youngsters, who are unfortunately less and less excited by cross-country racing with its harsh training demands, and who prefer to endlessly practice stunts and tricks. Jumps over natural obstacles and DIY ramps, fast downhill rides in disused quarries and bomb craters and trial manoeuvers over old cars and on steps cast a magical charm over young bikers. They invest all their pocket money in the newest parts and the right gear and spend the whole day on their bikes with no desire to go racing at all.

A Healthy Sport for All

The sales figures for mountain bikes show clearly that the sport of mountain bi-king is definitely not just for elite racers. Only a small fraction of the bikes purcha-sed are used for racing; the overwhelming majority is used for everyday off- and on-road riding.

Off-road mountain biking is a great sport for families with children because they can experience nature without being endangered by traffic. Driving often for miles at the weekend with the bikes on the car roof instead of riding there by bike is not ideal. Even right next to cities there are usually great locations that can be directly accessed by bike.

The environment should be respected, and mountain bikers should remain on tracks and paths to avoid disturbing the vegetation cover and wild animals in their shelters.

Mountain biking is a stimulating activity for mind and body as a keep-fit and rehab sport. The high number of gears on mountain bikes makes it easy to select the correct exercise intensity. Biking is also demanding in terms of coordination. Longer rides at low intensity on relatively flat terrain are an experience that every keep-fit cyclist can handle. An upright, but not stiff, sitting position and, if possi-ble, a suspension fork or a full suspension bike will considerably enhance the com-fort while riding.

Competitive Mountain Biking

The mountain racing scene has evolved from its initial stages when it was domina-ted by ex-racing cyclists and enthusiasts, and nowadays many mountain bikers are completely new to the sport.

Since the introduction of the World Cup, the sport has become very professional and more and more commercialized.

There are certainly no other sports that are as physically and mentally exhausting as a cross-country race over a tough course. Just being part of a mass start and the tension of jostling for a good starting position make your pulse race. During the race you are constantly riding at your performance limit, you are overtaken by other riders, you overtake some riders yourself, you stop yourself from being overtaken, and you may fall and try to ride through technically demanding passages as safely and as fast as possible. To succeed even at a regional level, you must have a lot of training under your belt, a fair amount of natural talent and, above all, be highly motivated to work hard and suffer in training.

The performance level in cross-country racing was really low from the early to mid-1980s, so that almost anyone could take part in international races, apart from

a few elite riders. Today, though, a broad, high-level elite with a professional approach to the sport has formed and explores every opportunity to succeed.

New young riders appear on the World Cup scene every year, dominate the racing scene for a short time and then disappear for a while. Most of these riders started out on the roads and are or were at least national-level road cycle racers.

Competitive mountain biking is now taken up by the first pure mountain bikers, meaning those who have not come to the sport via road cycling. However, in order to be able to keep up with the world's best, these riders also need to take part in road races and tours.

If we consider the professionalizing process initiated and forced by the World Cycling Association, which is so damaging to the sport at the lower levels of competition, it is noteworthy that in mountain biking performances are generally improving.

Once certain mountain bike races become so lucrative that they can compete with the classic road cycling races, strong road pros with thousands of racing miles in their legs will definitely also participate in these cross-country races, and as long as they can manage the technical aspect of the courses and train to race over shorter distances, they will always prevail over the current mountain bikers.

A similar phenomenon is noticeable in the sport of track cycling, which opened to professionals at the Olympic Games and World Championships. Suddenly, in the individual and team endurance disciplines and point races, the pros pulled away from the existing professional amateurs, setting incredible new world records in the process. This was and is possible because they were accustomed to events such as the great tour races, which require a completely different performance potential than would be possible in amateur cycling. A similar development is very likely to occur in mountain biking in the near future.

In the technical disciplines such as downhill, dual slalom and the different trial races, this development will not take place as they require other abilities rather than endurance and strength. Cycling technique and coordination must be trained equally intensively but are more strongly linked than endurance and strength to the rider's physical talent. It is usually not possible to make a trial rider out of a rider with poor coordination skills, whereas a merely average cross-country rider can go on to be very successful after years of well-planned training. In the technical disciplines, performance progress is increasingly dependent on equipment innovation and is often the limiting factor, at least in downhill and dual slalom.

2   The Physiology and Anatomy of a Mountain Biker

2.1   From Beginner to Pro From a Physiological Perspective

For an individual with little endurance background, mountain biking will trigger certain changes in the body. The purpose of these changes is to adapt the body to increased performance demands. In addition to visible changes, such as more defined muscles or weight loss, a series of other more subtle adaptation processes take place, which increase the performance level of the body's complex system.

For a mountain biker who takes his hobby seriously, learning as much about the body as possible should be a fundamental requirement because it enables him to do the sport he loves. An understanding and awareness of the body are becoming less and less emphasized in a time of computer-controlled training, and an unavoidable consequence of this is that many elite athletes overtrain until their bodies break down.

This chapter presents the anatomical and physiological basics relevant to the endurance sport mountain biking. It also looks at the adaptation processes caused by endurance training and should help the mountain biker to understand the physical processes, injuries and also performance improvement. This knowledge will also provide a basic understanding of training and all associated factors.

There is not enough room to explore these topics in great detail, but interested readers can always consult good anatomy and physiology books to find more in-depth descriptions.

2.1.1   Training Effects on the Heart, Circulation and Musculoskeletal System

The body's adaptation process is divided into two phases. During the first phase, at low training volumes and intensities (i.e., at grass roots and rehab level), there is just a functional adaptation that is characterized by an improved metabolism and a corresponding increase in the economy of the cardiovascular system.

The second adaptation phase is dimensional adaptation, during which the size of the internal organs changes.

The heart becomes more efficient.

Regular, long-term endurance training leads to an adaptation process in the heart that results in what is known as athlete's heart, characterized by an increase in size and a resulting drop in heart rate. This adaptation process is a result of the faster metabolism, especially in the muscles, in which increased oxygen and nutritional requirements can only be met by a greater blood circulation, requiring a more efficient heart. While an untrained heart weighs about 10.6 ounces (300 g), that of an endurance athlete can weigh up to 17.6 ounces (500 g). This increase in weight is accompanied by an increase in size. From about 800 ml for men and 500 ml for women, heart size can increase up to 900–1200 milliliters, and in rare cases up to 1500 milliliters. The largest hearts can be found in road racing cyclists and are the result of their often extreme endurance training loads.

The increase in heart volume enables a greater stroke volume. The stroke volume is the amount of blood that the heart pumps into the aorta per beat (80 ml for the untrained and up to 150 ml for trained endurance athletes). However, as the body does not need more blood for the same performance, the heart can pump more slowly. The maximum possible cardiac output per minute (i.e., the total amount of blood pumped by the left side of the heart per minute [heart rate x stroke volume; e.g., 70 x 80 ml = 5.6 l/min at rest]), rises in a trained athlete compared to an untrained person so that the muscles have more blood available to them per unit of time. The maximum heart rate increases only minimally after years of endurance training, so the greater maximum stroke volume produces a greatly increased maximum cardiac output per minute.

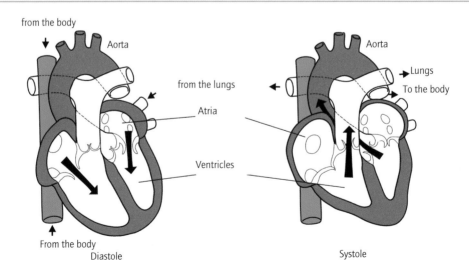

Fig. 2.1: Anatomy and the cardiac cycle

At maximum effort, the untrained individual attains a cardiac output of about 20 liters, while someone with endurance training can attain values of over 30 liters. The maximum heart rate is usually calculated by the formula 220 – age, which should be treated as an approximate figure and is therefore practically useless at elite level. There is more on the determining and importance of maximum heart rate in chapter 3.

A clear indicator of athlete's heart is a lowered heart rate from about 60–70 (70–80 for women) bpm for the untrained athlete to 40–50 bpm at high performance level. At pro level, resting heart rates of below 40 bpm are common and may occasionally be as low as 30 bpm.

Training should never just stop completely once your mountain biking career is over, as this can cause the heart to suffer potentially dangerous training withdrawal symptoms.
 The heart's function is illustrated in figure 2.1.

The advantages of athlete's heart:
 * greater efficiency
 * the same performance can be achieved with a lower heart rate lower resting and working heart rate, which protects the heart (comparable to lower revs in a car)
 * economizing the circulatory system
 * other positive physical adaptation processes take place during the development of athlete's heart

Vascular System

Oxygen-rich blood is sent round the body via the aorta, the arteries and the arterioles. The arterioles and capillaries of the muscles are actively constricted at rest, thereby preventing unnecessary blood supply to the muscles because at rest other organs require the blood (e.g., gastro-intestinal tract, kidneys, liver).

When a person starts to move, the blood vessels in the working muscles expand to allow more blood, and therefore more oxygen and nutrients, to flow into the muscle fibers. There is therefore a corresponding reduction in blood flow to the digestive system during exercise. The heart pumps harder to meet the muscles' increased demand for blood.

The capillaries, the smallest blood vessels and also where oxygen exchange takes place (oxygen $\longleftrightarrow$ carbon dioxide, nutrients $\longleftrightarrow$ metabolites), are connected to the venules and ultimately to the veins, which join either the superior or inferior vena cava. The veins transport the blood back to the heart.

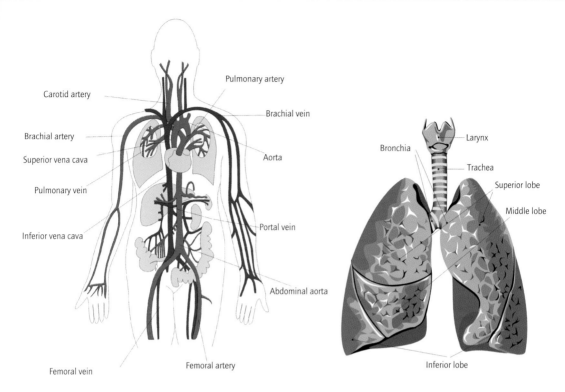

Fig. 2.2: Circulatory system   Fig. 2.3: Anatomy of the lungs

Respiration

Oxygen-poor, carbon-dioxide-rich blood flows into the alveoli, the extremely thin-walled capillaries inside the lungs, where it releases its carbon dioxide and absorbs oxygen. This process is called external respiration, while the exchange of substances between the blood and the body cells is called internal respiration.

With the aid of the breathing muscles, primarily the diaphragm, at rest the lungs expand during inhalation, air flows down the trachea and bronchia into the pulmonary alveoli where the gaseous exchange takes place, and finally the carbon dioxide air escapes from the lungs (exhalation). Only during exercise (e.g., cycling)—when breathing is heavier—is the diaphragm breathing supported by chest breathing. A whole series of auxiliary respiratory muscles then reinforce the inhalation and exhalation processes and increase the energy requirement of the respiratory muscles up to 10% of the total energy requirement. During exercise, the oxygen requirement of these muscles increases to up to 15–20% of the maximum oxygen intake.

At rest, for each breath, only about 0.5 liters of air is breathed in and out 15 times per minute (= 7.5 l); while at maximum effort, the trained mountain biker may after a finishing sprint, for example, inhale and exhale over 190 liters of air per minute.

The vital capacity (the maximum amount of air that a person can expel from the lungs after first filling the lungs to their maximum) is highly dependent on age, sex and body size. The vital capacity is usually between three and seven liters, but it reveals little about a mountain biker's absolute endurance ability. The elite African distance runners, for example, have small lungs compared to Europeans but still usually run faster.

Blood

The 5–6 liters of blood in our bodies contain roughly 55% blood plasma (fluid) and about 45% various blood cells. Blood accounts for about 5–6% of our body-weight. Endurance training, such as mountain biking, increases blood volume by about 15%.

These are the main functions attributed to blood:
- transport (oxygen, carbon dioxide, nutrients, metabolic waste, hormones),
- the transportation and circulation of heat,
- clotting and
- immune defense.

1 mm³ of blood (i.e., a tiny amount) contains an incredible 4.5–5 million red blood corpuscles and about 5,000–8,000 white blood corpuscles for immune defense. 100 milliliters of blood also contains about 7 grams of protein. The red blood corpuscles (erythrocytes) are responsible for transporting oxygen and carbon dioxide.

The hematocrit value shows the volume percentage of blood cells in the blood. Hematocrit is now often used as proof of the commonly used doping agent (especially in road cycling) erythropoietin (EPO). EPO increases the production of red blood cells, which enables the athlete to absorb more oxygen. The result is not only a significantly higher performance level, but also a significantly higher risk of dying of deep vein thrombosis (blood clot). The sport of road cycling, where this doping method is still more commonly abused than in mountain biking, has already witnessed a series of sudden deaths that have been traced to the consumption of this hormone.

Maximum Oxygen Uptake

Maximum oxygen uptake **(VO$_2$max)** is a very interesting physiological measurement, for it is the principal method of measuring endurance ability. VO$_2$max is the greatest possible amount of oxygen—not breath—that the mountain biker can inhale under maximum loading conditions by his lungs into his blood.

The way to measure the VO_2max accurately is on an exercise bike as part of a performance test. The normal value for an untrained person is roughly 3 l oxygen per minute and can be increased by appropriate training to 5–6 liters per minute. The VO_2max is dependent on the athlete's fitness, age, sex and weight. For example, a heavier person will need more oxygen for the same external performance than a lighter person, because he has more bodyweight to move. For this reason, the weight-related VO_2max is used in order to obtain an accurate measurement of performance potential and to compare different athletes. The weight-related or relative VO_2max gives the oxygen intake per kilogram bodyweight and minute. The pros can attain values of over 80 milliliters oxygen per minute and kilogram bodyweight; untrained 20–30-year-olds, on the other hand, only reach 40–45 millileters per kilogram bodyweight and minute. The maximum oxygen intake for an untrained male declines by 1% per year, while women only lose 0.8 milliliters per year. However, most sedentary individuals do not know that this process can be stopped and even reversed through endurance training. A fit 70-year-old can still attain the same results as an untrained 30-year-old.

Factors that influence VO_2max (as well as age, weight and sex):
- the circulation transportation capacity (cardiac output),
- the oxygen transportation capacity of the blood,
- respiration and gas exchange in the lungs,
- blood supply to the muscles (capillarization) and
- intramuscular metabolism (enzyme loading).

Musculoskeletal System

Muscles

The approximately 430 muscles in the human body normally account for between 40 and 45% of its bodyweight and require about 20% of its resting energy expenditure. During maximum effort (peak sporting performance), this value increases up to up to 90%. Muscles are able to convert chemical energy (nutrients) into mechanical energy (contraction), like an internal combustion engine.

A muscle or a muscle group never works alone during a movement but is always dependent on one or more antagonists, such as the hamstrings (agonists) and quadriceps (antagonists) in the leg work counter to each other.

All the major muscles in the human body are shown in figures 2.4–2.7. These illustrations should be referred to when reading chapters 4 (strength training) and 5 (stretching), which feature detailed descriptions of individual muscles. The comments on the illustrations contain the English and Latin muscle names and a mountain-bike-specific description of their functions.

Torso

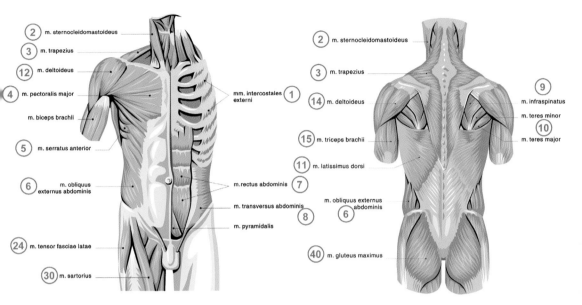

Fig. 2.4: Diagram of the muscles of the torso, showing the main muscles (left: anterior view of the torso; right: posterior view of the torso)

1. **mm. intercostales externi (external intercostals)**: *auxiliary respiratory muscles used for chest (thoracic) breathing.*
2. **m. sternocleidomastoideus (sternocleidomastoid or SCM)**: *turns the head to the side (e.g., when looking around on the bike).*
3. **m. trapezius (trapezius)**: *has three functional areas: it raises and supports the shoulders and stabilizes the shoulder blades; it raises the shoulders when you ride out of the saddle.*
4. **m. pectoralis major (pecs)**: *pulls the arm toward the body; used in cycling eccentrically during strenuous downhill rides and concentrically when riding out of the saddle.*
5. **m. serratus anterior (serratus anterior)**: *pulls the shoulder blades forward and allows the arm to be raised above the horizontal; slightly involved in shock absorption.*
6. **m. obliquus externus abdominis (obliques)**: *lateral turning and bending of the torso; stabilizing the hips when cycling, supporting the pulling action when riding out of the saddle.*
7. **m. rectus abdominis (abs or "six pack")**: *bends the torso forwards, stabilizes the pelvis when pedaling; part of the muscle loop used in powerful pedaling.*
8. **m. transversus abdominis (TVA)**: *helps to compress the ribs and viscera, providing thoracic and pelvic stability.*
9. **m. infraspinatus (infraspinatus)**: *externally rotates the arm and stabilizes the shoulder joint; used in shock absorption on rough terrain; one of the four muscles of the rotator cuff.*
10. **m. teres major/minor**: *turn the arm outward and pull it toward the torso; used when riding uphill out of the saddle.*
11. **m. latissimus dorsi (lats)**: *pulls raised arms down toward the body.*
12. **m. erector spinae (spinal erector)**: *not illustrated; deep muscle that runs alongside the vertebral column; holds the back erect and straightens it; holds the back in place when pedaling.*
13. **mm. suboccipitales**: *deeper muscles, not illustrated, turn the head.*

Arms

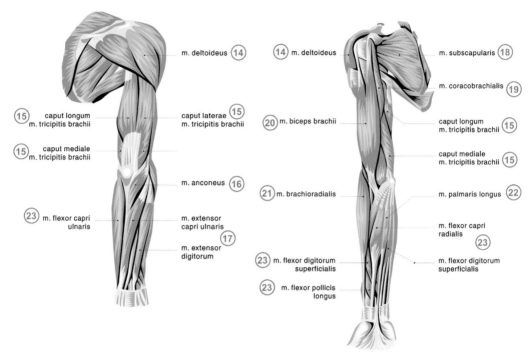

Fig. 2.5: Diagram of the muscles of the right arm—the most important muscles are named (left: posterior view with elbow; right: anterior view with elbow)

14. *m. deltoideus* (deltoid): *different parts of the muscle raises the arm to the front, side and rear; used when riding out of the saddle uphill and in downhill racing.*

15. *m. triceps brachii* (triceps): *extends the arm at the elbow; important shock absorber in downhill riding, where it works eccentrically.*

16. *m. anconaeus* (anconaeus): *assists in the extension of the elbow; functions like the triceps.*

17. *mm. extensor carpi/digitorum: extends the wrist and the fingers; used to grip the handle bars and for shock absorption.*

18. *m. subscapularis* (subscapularis): *stabilizes the shoulder joint and turns the arm in toward the body.*

19. *m. coracobrachialis* (coracobrachialis): *raises the arm, stabilizes the shoulder joint during heavy loading.*

20. *m. biceps brachii* (biceps): *flexes the arm at the elbow; used when riding out of the saddle uphill and on the flat and also when seated.*

21. *m. brachioradialis* (brachioradialis): *flexes the arm at the elbow; used when riding uphill and also when seated.*

22. *m. palmaris longus* (palmaris longus): *finger flexor; used to grip the handlebar.*

23. *mm. flexor carpi/digitorum: finger and wrist flexor; mainly used concentrically to grip the handlebar.*

Leg – Anterior View

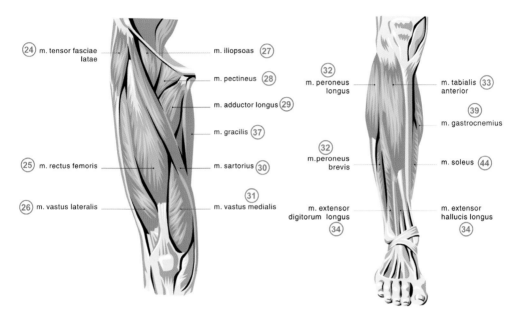

Fig. 2.6: Diagram of the muscles of the front of the leg with the most important muscles named (right leg)

24. *m. tensor fasciae latae* (TFL): *hip abductor muscle; used in the upward phase of the pedaling action.*

25. *m. rectus femoris* (one of the four quad muscles): *knee extensor and hip flexor; used concentrically in the downward phase of the pedaling action.*

26. *m. vastus lateralis* (largest of the four quad muscles): *extends and stabilizes the knee, also flexes the hips; used concentrically in the downward phase of the pedaling action.*

27. *m. iliopsoas* (psoas): *the strongest of the hip flexor muscles; part of the muscle loop used in vigorous pedaling.*

28. *m. pectineus* (hip flexors): *flexes the hip; used in the upward phase of the pedaling action.*

29. *m. adductor longus* (adductor): *adducts the thigh (i.e., brings the thigh closer to the middle sagittal plane of the body) and supports flexion.*

30. *m. sartorius* (tailor's muscle): *hip flexor; turns the lower leg inward and the thigh outward; supports knee flexion.*

31. *m. vastus medialis* (teardrop muscle, one of the quads): *extends and stabilizes the knee joint, also hip flexor; used concentrically in the downward pedaling action.*

32. *mm. peronaeus longus/brevis: raise and evert (turn out) the foot; support the ankle extensors; solicited in the upward movement of the pedals before the upper "dead point" (pulling).*

33. *m. tibialis anterior* (shin muscle): *raises the foot; used in the upward movement of the pedals before the upper "dead point" (pulling).*

34. *m. extensor digitorum: extends the toes; used in the upward phase of the pedaling action (pulling).*

Leg – Posterior View

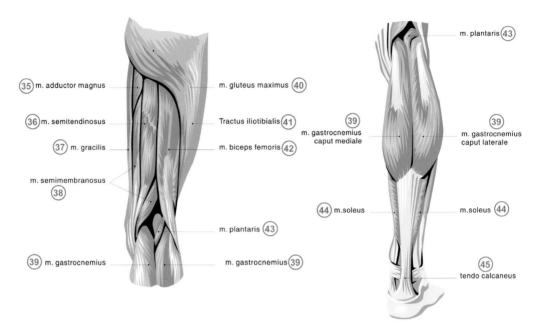

Fig. 2.7: Diagram of the rear leg muscles with the most important muscles named (right leg)

35. *m. adductor magnus:* adductor of the thigh (i.e., pulls the thigh into the midline of the body) and extends the hips; used in the leg extension element of the pedaling cycle.

36. *m. semitendinosus:* knee flexor and hip extensor; particularly important in the flexion phase of the rear pedaling cycle.

37. *m. gracilis:* hip and knee flexor; used in the upward element of the pedaling action.

38. *m. semimembranosus:* knee flexor and hip extensor; particularly important in the flexion of the rear pedaling cycle.

39. *m. gastrocnemius* (calf muscle): ankle extensor and knee flexor; mainly used in downward pedaling action but also when pulling the pedal up.

40. *m. glutaeus maximus* (glutes): hip extensor; powerful supporter of the quadriceps in leg extension, front phase of the pedaling cycle.

41. *m. tractus iliotibialis* (iliotibial tract or band, IT band): not a muscle but a connective tissue, thickening or reinforcing the muscle fasciae surrounding and reinforcing the femur.

42. *m. biceps femoris* (long-head muscle): knee flexor and abductor; hip extensor, especially in the flexion phase of the rear pedaling cycle but also important as a hip extensor in the front pedaling cycle.

43. *m. plantaris:* insignificant role in the pedaling cycle.

44. *m. soleus* (calf): ankle extensor; solicited in pedaling action, supports the calf muscle.

45. *tendo calcaneus* (Achilles tendon): connects the muscles of the calf to the ankle.

There are basically two different types of muscle function: a) static and b) dynamic. Static means stationary, and in mountain biking these are the muscles that are responsible for maintaining posture. The muscles of the arm, the back of the neck and the back are responsible for holding the head and upper body in place when sitting still and, therefore, mainly work statically. The pedaling process on the other hand is a dynamic action, which means that the muscles actually shorten when they contract to overcome a load. The opposite, eccentric loading (yielding), takes place when landing after jumping off a wall when the legs must give, and although the muscles resist, they are still stretched (lengthening).

The exclusively concentric pedaling action in the principal leg muscles is why mountain bikers suffer from muscle soreness after riding an unfamiliar course (e.g., a cross-country race). The extensor muscles of the leg are vigorously stretched in the eccentric loading phase of the race (absorption of bodyweight), and the cyclist's body is unaccustomed to this stretching. This causes microscopic muscle tears (microtrauma), which are the cause of muscle soreness. This is one reason why mountain bikers should also regularly undertake running training.

The muscles of the human body contain slow- and fast-twitch muscle fibers and a hybrid type. The slow, red muscle fibers are endurance fibers, and these fibers are mainly solicited during mountain biking (70–90%). Fast-twitch or white muscle fibers are thicker and tire more quickly and are more commonly found in speed-strength and speed athletes.

Untrained people have a mixture of all three types and proportion depends on their body type. Limits can only be changed by training. The process by which white fibers are converted to red or vice versa is still not fully understood, but it is clear that the type of exercise performed (endurance or strength) is probably what triggers the change. It is easier to convert fast-twitch fibers to slow-twitch than the other way around, so it is therefore considerably easier to reach a good endurance level through training than a good sprinting level. It is also true that youngsters with a high percentage of endurance fibers are more likely to specialize in the endurance disciplines where they will be more successful. This is certainly more noticeable in the speed-strength events, although these choices are not made according to muscle fiber distribution. Instead, the selection process is a natural one based on performance.

Endurance training improves the capillarization (the amount of capillaries per muscle fiber) of the muscle tissue, which means that the metabolic and gas exchange surfaces between the muscle fibers and the blood increase in size, thus enabling the metabolism to work faster and more economically.

Bones

The bones in the human body are lightweight; a solid external compact layer surrounds the spongy-looking internal layer. Bones are relatively elastic despite their stiff and inflexible appearance. Pulling, pushing, bending and stretching are tolerated to an amazing extent. Mountain biking is a low-impact sport that is gentle on the bones and joints, unlike running, for example. Cycling can even strengthen bone structure, particularly in the legs.

Joints

The ends of the bones are covered in cartilage, and they meet to form joints, which provide flexibility. Joints are composed of two or, more rarely, three bones, which are connected by tendons, muscles, capsules and ligaments. The cartilage-covered bone ends form the joint surfaces inside the joint. Cartilage is a very resilient, smooth substance with a durability that surpasses any man-made substitute. It encloses the joint cavity—the space between the bone ends—with a two-layered capsule, which first gives additional support to the joint and then produces what is called synovial fluid.

Digestion

The digestive process can be explained from ingestion to excretion using the example of a muesli bar. The times given are a rough guide only and may differ considerably depending on situation and circumstance.

3:30 pm: A test cyclist starts a three to four hour training ride. His last meal was not a big one, eaten three hours before.
5:00:   The cyclist eats a muesli bar. He breaks it down mechanically using his teeth, and his saliva turns it into a slippery pulp ("bolus" or "chyme"). [1] Saliva enzymes in the mouth already start to break down the complex carbohydrates.
5:01:   The muesli bolus travels down the esophagus (gullet) to the stomach. Peristalsis (muscle contractions) helps to accelerate it down the 11-inches (30 cm) long esophagus. [2]
5:02:   Now in the stomach, the muesli bar triggers the production of hydrochloric acid and enzymes, which chemically process the bolus into gastric juice. [3] Roughly 1.5–2 liters of gastric juice is produced daily. Only fats and proteins are attacked by the enzymes; carbohydrates are not broken down any further here. The hydrochloric acid continues to break down the rough muesli bolus.

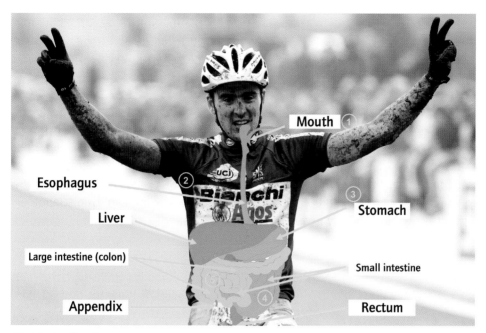

Fig. 2.8: The digestive system

5:03: Water secretion dilutes the chyme, which is mixed up thoroughly by the movements of the stomach wall like a cement mixer. At fast cycling speeds, the body wastes no energy on digestion, and the digestive process is postponed until a more gentle stage of the ride.

5:09: The stomach continues to work like a mixer; slowly the fats rise to the surface of the chyme, while the carbohydrates are deposited on the stomach fundus.

5:25: The chyme is further diluted and now only takes a few minutes to leave the stomach. High-carbohydrate drinks would already be in the intestine.

5:40: Finally, just before the cyclist hits the "wall," the stomach opens its pyloric sphincter at its lower end and allows the chyme to gradually enter the duodenum. The pancreas secretes enzymes to break down carbohydrates, proteins and fats into the duodenum, and the secretion of bile acid for fat digestion also starts.

5:43: Rhythmic (peristaltic) movements push the muesli bar into the adjacent small intestine. The complex carbohydrates broken down into glucose are now absorbed into the blood via the villi that protrude from the lining of the intestine and make their way toward the liver via the portal vein system. Part of the fat has already been broken down into fatty acids and glycerin. Also the proteins have, in the meantime, been broken down into individual amino acids. Their absorption (resorption) starts gradually.

5:46: The chyme travels farther down the small intestine, the top third of which mainly serves to absorb glucose. 4 The glucose travels to the liver via the portal vein system, where the glucose molecules are turned into glycogen. Some of the glycogen is stored in the liver itself (size of the deposit: 100–130 g glycogen), while the rest travels to the muscles where it is either stored or burned immediately. Also the amino acids, fatty acids, vitamins A, B, C, E and K and the minerals are absorbed into the blood from the small intestine.

6:30: Remains of the muesli can still be found in the small intestine.

7:00: End of the training ride. Almost all of the glucose has now been resorbed, and the proteins have also been partially absorbed. Fat digestion and resorption takes a while longer.

7:30: The process starts again as the cyclist eats his evening meal. The amino acids from the bar have now reached the liver, where they are reassembled into proteins known as plasma protein and travel into the blood. Excess protein (in the case of excessive calorie consumption or lack of food) are burned off or converted into fat and stored (see chapter 7).

10:30: The rest of the muesli bar leaves the small intestine for the rectum. 5 Eighty to ninety percent of the nutrients have now been removed from the chyme. In the colon, the water used for digestion must be removed. This means that the consistency of the chyme becomes thicker and drier as it passes through the colon. At the top of the colon, more minerals and remaining nutrients are absorbed.

The next morning
The muesli bar leaves the body in the form of feces. Fatty foods would take about 10 hours longer to digest.

Nervous System

Every single physical process and action is governed by the nervous system, partly consciously and partly unconsciously. The nervous system senses, processes and reacts to stimuli with the aid of the sensory and effector organs that enable us to interact with the world. The nervous system consists of many billions of cells that have lost the ability to divide.

From an anatomical point of view, we distinguish between the central nervous system (CNS: brain and spinal cord) and the peripheral nervous system (PNS) with the nerves that represent the connection to the sensory and effector organs. From a functional point of view, we differentiate between the voluntary (somatic) and involuntary (autonomic) nervous systems.

The somatic nervous system carries all voluntary movement commands to the corresponding effector organs, usually muscles.

While the brain is the control center of the nervous system, the spinal cord is the wiring system responsible for transferring information to and from the effector organs along the nerves running down the spinal cord, which is protected by the vertebrae. Secondly, like the brain, the spinal cord is the nerve center for subordinate processes, such as the reflexes.

The autonomic nervous system, which controls all unconscious processes in the body, consists of two different sub-systems. These sub-systems have completely different areas of activity. The parasympathetic nervous system is responsible for all physical functions when at rest (digestion, recovery). The sympathetic nervous system, on the other hand, controls physical activity and boosts the mobilization of the organ system responsible for movement.

Kidneys

The kidneys have a very important role in the body as blood filters and excretory organs. In the case of cycling, they have to work overtime because their filtering action has to keep pace with the increased calorie burning associated with physical exercise. Kidneys eliminate salts, metabolites of the protein metabolism process, water and also foreign substances from the blood and from the body. From the 1,500 liters of blood that flow through the kidneys on a daily basis, about 150 liters of primary urine is filtered, which eventually is concentrated into about 1.5 liters of urine and eliminated.

2.1.2 Metabolism

Contrary to the belief that the heart and circulatory system limit performance, the real bottleneck of performance development is actually muscle metabolism. Only the contractile elements of the body (muscles) are in the position to transform chemical energy into mechanical energy, thereby permitting the body to move. As such, the metabolism, structure and control (coordination) of the muscles are the performance-limiting factors in mountain biking.

The muscles provide energy by three metabolic pathways, which are presented here separately for the sake of clarity but actually interlink like gear wheels. The transitions from one type of energy metabolism to another are smooth. The main types are aerobic energy supply and the anaerobic energy supply, which is further divided into the anaerobic alactic and anaerobic lactic energy supply.

Aerobic Energy Supply (Aerobic Glycolysis and Lipolysis)

What does aerobic mean? Aerobic means that energy is supplied with the aid of oxygen. Aer comes from the Greek word meaning air. For the mountain biker, the aerobic energy supply is the most important metabolic pathway as it can work for long periods of time, supply relatively high amounts of energy and even restore and regenerate both anaerobic metabolic pathways after they are used up.

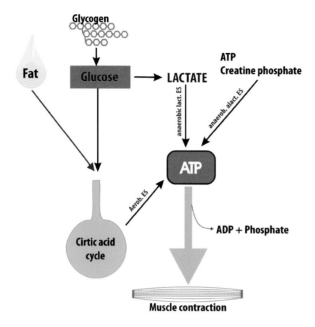

Fig. 2.9: Simplified diagram the chemical energy to mechanical energy conversion

In the aerobic metabolism, fats and carbohydrates are burned or oxidized. The most important fuel is glucose (aerobic glycolysis), a simple carbohydrate with the chemical formula $C6H12O6$. Glucose is the by-product of the complex carbohydrates (see chapter 7, Nutrition).

Very broken-down, the glucose combines with oxygen and is split into carbon dioxide (exhaled from the lungs) and water. A relatively large amount of energy in the form of ATP (adenosine triphosphate, a very energy-rich molecule) is released in the process.

ATP Fuels Contraction

ATP is the direct energy store of the cells and is used as muscle fuel, which ultimately triggers muscle contractions. By splitting off of a phosphate group, only ATP is capable of triggering a muscle contraction on a molecular level because of the attachment, pivoting and detachment of structures called myosin heads. However, ATP must already be present at the appropriate attachment points so that the muscle is ready to be deployed at any time. If the muscle cells' ATP supply is running low, especially if there is no new synthesis, the connections between the contractile structures do not loosen, and the muscle stiffens. This can be seen, for example, in the state of rigor mortis. In the case of mountain bikers, cramps, especially in the leg muscles, are a sign of increasing exhaustion and a lack of ATP in the muscle fibers, because the connections are no longer able to separate. The layperson usually attributes this to a lack of magnesium, as magnesium enables the splitting of ATP into ADP. Very often, though, cramps are just a sign of overexertion and exhausted ATP reserves and are therefore an energy problem that will disappear with improved fitness. In the muscle fibers, all conversion processes of high-energy foodstuffs are ultimately designed to ensure ATP production.

Simplified Diagram of Energy Supply

The energy supply system can be compared to a steam engine. The fuels (fats and glucose) represent water; the fire, sometimes smaller, sometimes larger, represents the metabolic pathway.

The steam created from water represents the ATP. In order to move or drive something forward, the cell requires ATP, just as the steam engine requires steam. As the body's ATP store is limited, so is the steam store in the engine's boiler, meaning that it must constantly be stoked.

Aerobic energy is generated in the muscle fiber, specifically the mitochondria, and referred to as the power station of the cell. The glucose is either transported away in the blood and broken down or comes from the glycogen reserves in the cells (glycogen is the storage form of glucose) where it is transported after conversion and splitting processes in the mitochondria.

Fat Metabolism (Lipolysis)

Fats, as well as carbohydrates, are also burned on the aerobic pathway. This process is called *lipolysis*. Fats are composed of glycerol and fatty acids. The fatty acids are integrated into a certain place in the carbohydrate metabolism and burned together with the carbohydrates. For this reason, energy from fats can only be made useable when carbohydrates are being burned. Carnitine is required for the permeation of fatty acid co-enzyme A (produced from the fatty acids) in the mitochondria. However, research into the performance-enhancing effects of carnitine supplements has proved inconclusive.

The disadvantage of fat-burning is that it is only available at very low exercise intensities, as a lot of oxygen is required. The stored energy or the calorific value for fats are double that of carbohydrates, (i.e., 9.3 kcal to 4.1 kcal per g).

The fat metabolism (lipolysis) of the mountain biker must be trained in order to protect the heavily performance-limiting glycogen reserves, which after about two hours of intensive exercise are mostly empty. While the untrained person can cover about 40% of the required energy at average intensity using the fat metabolism, for the endurance-trained mountain biker this figure is 60% and higher. With increasing stamina levels, at the same intensity the proportion of fats at energy generation increases. The precious glycogen reserves are thereby protected and saved for race-deciding high-intensity spurts. The endurance-trained mountain biker can store two to three times more fat in the muscle cells for energy production than the untrained person.

Glycogen Reserves

If basic endurance is not at a high level, the muscle cells already start to draw on the glycogen at relatively low training loads. Between 400 and 500 grams of glycogen are stored in the liver and muscles, with the majority being in the muscles.

An important factor in cycling performance is the levels of stored muscle glycogen. If the glycogen reserves are empty after the race, they must be refilled, which takes between 24 and 48 hours even with an optimum diet (see chapter 7, Nutrition).

Endurance training improves the metabolic situation in the muscle fibers themselves. The enzyme content in the mitochondria is higher and the substrates (e.g., glucose, fatty acids) exist in higher concentrations ready to be broken down than in the untrained individual. Also the number of mitochondria per fiber increases and oxygen can be used more easily and in greater amounts thanks to improved capillarization (i.e., number of capillaries per muscle fiber). Therefore aerobic metabolism is carried out faster and more economically.

Anaerobic Energy Supply

a) Anaerobic lactic acid energy supply (anaerobic glycolysis)

Anaerobic means energy supply without oxygen. On this metabolic pathway, lactate, or lactic acid, is produced, hence the name lactic acid energy supply. Lactate causes the hyperacidity of the muscles and quickly causes an enforced rest. The muscles always use the metabolic pathway when aerobic combustion as an energy source is insufficient in order to execute the required performance.

In the cells, glucose is split into lactate in the absence of oxygen. This continues until the glycolytic enzyme responsible for the splitting is limited by the hyperacidity caused by the lactate and stops working. As glucose splits off, energy is again released in the form of ATP. The remaining lactate also enters the blood stream shortly afterward, where the concentration can be determined for performance testing purposes. The accumulated lactate is partially resynthesized into glucose in the liver or metabolized by the heart muscle.

It is amazing that the anaerobic splitting of a glucose molecule only provides about 5% of the combustion energy of the aerobic pathway, also blocks the lactic acid energy supply itself and nevertheless manages to supply a higher amount of energy per unit of time. This is because theoretically an unlimited number of glucose molecules can be split at the same time, and their total energy is able to ensure a very high performance output for a relatively short time of 40–60 seconds.

Metabolism During Exercise

At the start of a ride, particularly a race, the aerobic energy supply is not yet running optimally, especially if the rider has not warmed up sufficiently. In this case, by going into oxygen debt, the energy deficit is covered by the anaerobic lactic acid pathway.

First priority: a post-race drink, but the right kind!

The resulting lactic acid is called warm-up lactate, and it is burned away once the aerobic metabolism kicks in. Lactate also builds up during intermediate sprints or attacks. However, if the lactate production exceeds a certain point at which the lactate concentration is so high that it blocks the other metabolic pathways and the lactate can no longer be burned on the aerobic pathway, the rider will be forced to drop due to muscle hyperacidity.

In the initial stages of a movement, the first seconds are covered by the ATP/CP pool and only then, depending on exercise intensity, is the anaerobic metabolism used. As mentioned, the three described metabolic processes do not take place in isolation; they are strongly interconnected and affect and enable each other. Muscle work is in this way enabled through the following energy supply sequence: ATP–CP–anaerobic glycolysis–aerobic glycolysis, lipolysis. These processes cascade from one to the other at the start of exercise. *Figure 2.10* illustrates the approximate chronology of the processes.

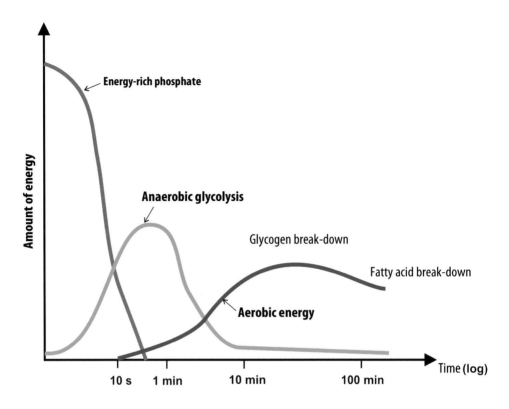

Fig. 2.10: Types of energy production related to exercise duration

Protein Metabolism

If energy reserves are unable to meet the demands of long, intensive training rides and races, the body draws on its own structures and metabolizes protein. These catabolic phases in which the body itself is broken down can be very damaging, and recovery requires weeks of reduced training. Typically, they occur due to glycogen depletion caused by a poor diet and hard training (see chapter 7 Nutrition). In unevenly-matched training groups, the weakest (youngsters) tend to be affected, as they often have a tendency to overtrain.

b) Anaerobic alactic energy supply

The anaerobic alactic energy supply only plays a subordinate role for mountain bikers, although it is vital for strength athletes like weightlifters, shot-putters and also for those who practice jumping events. Alactic means that, unlike the anaerobic lactic acid energy supply mentioned above, no lactate is created.

The ATP and creatine phosphate reserves (energy-rich phosphate compound) are used up for this maximum five- to eight-second energy supply type, which unfortunately suffices for only a few, maximum muscle contractions.

It is important to understand that ATP is essential for every muscle contraction; without ATP the muscles cannot contract. For this reason, cells' ATP reserves must constantly be replenished, predominantly on the aerobic metabolic pathway. Also ATP is necessary for other energy-consuming processes in the cells, such as recovery processes or cell growth.

When a phosphate residue is split off from ATP, the stored energy is released and the muscle contracts. The remaining ADP (adenosine diphosphate) is later recycled into ATP when a phosphate residue is split from creatine phosphate.

By sets of short, maximum sprint loads lasting about eight seconds, the CP reserves can be increased, which is very beneficial for mountain bikers especially during inclines or accelerations (e.g., attacks or after curves). The importance of these energy reserves, even in endurance sports, has been increasingly recognized.

Metabolic Phases
In endurance sports and in mountain biking, we can distinguish between four different metabolic phases. Below, these phases are described briefly in the context of a step test on an exercise bike.

First Phase

At low loading, the metabolic pathway is aerobic, and mainly fat is metabolized. The lactate levels are similar to or slightly lower than resting levels and therefore give no indication of exercise intensity.

Second Phase

With increasing exercise intensity, the proportion of metabolized carbohydrate increases. In this zone, lactate levels are slightly raised, but they do not rise any farther if the exercise intensity remains the same. As exercise intensity increases, anaerobic glycolysis provides an increasing proportion of the metabolism. As long as lactate elimination and production remain in equilibrium, a steady state exists. The maximum lactate steady state indicates the highest loading at which a balance between lactate elimination and production exists. This point is often compared to the anaerobic threshold and therefore defines the upper limit of the second phase.

Third Phase

In the third phase, if exercise intensity is constant, lactate accumulates in the blood, accompanied by rising lactate levels as more lactate is produced than can be eliminated. The proportion of anaerobic glycolysis in the energy supply is already very high now.

Fourth Phase

In the fourth phase, the energy supply is covered exclusively on the anaerobic pathway by anaerobic glycolysis. The highest lactate levels can be measured shortly after exercise breaks.

The difference Between Beginners and Pros

It is obvious from the previous chapter just how big the difference is between a mountain bike beginner, a cross-country cyclist who has been training for a year, and a professional cyclist. The pro is superior in all performance-physiological criteria thanks to an adaptation process over many years. If pros race against amateurs, the result is easy to predict, just as it would be for a Sedan racing in Formula 1.

Nina Göhl, Albstadt 2007

2.2 Requirement Profiles for Individual Disciplines

A requirement profile for each sport is essential for planning and monitoring training for both competitive and recreational athletes. It reveals the exact performance structure for a specific sport or activity. The performance structure is determined by performance factors, mainly fitness performance factors: strength, endurance, speed, flexibility and coordination. Also taken into account are the sport-specific performance-physiological features, the differing demands of racing and training, and also a profile of psychological, cognitive and social performance factors. Finally, do not neglect external performance factors such as course profile or distance and equipment factors, including the mountain bike and all other biking gear.

Mountain biking performance factors:
- Fitness
- Mental
- Cognitive
- Social
- External
- Equipment

In mountain biking, the rudimentary requirement profile drawn up by sports scientists has been refined and amended by the many studies since published on the subject.

In the context of this training book, the requirement profiles for each mountain bike discipline are outlined, paying particular attention to the performance-physiological factors. The profiles are not exhaustive, but are very useful when it comes to drawing up training plans.

One part of the performance factors is relevant for all mountain bike disciplines and is explained in the following section on cross-country:

2.2.1 Cross-Country

External Factors
Cross-country is undoubtedly the most popular of the mountain biking disciplines and therefore has the most participants, from elite level to grass-roots level racers. At elite level, circuit races with differing lap lengths should be distinguished from the rarer course races (point-to-point races).

Cross-country: At the start of the race the riders are packed tightly together (Sallhausen, 2011)

These often include marathons, which are special case, not just because of their length, and are discussed in section **2.2.2**.

The races rarely last more than three hours (only true for the later finishers; the fastest rarely take more than two hours, and since in the 2011 season when races were shortened, usually well under two hours), so the races fall into the category of long endurance III or long endurance II (up to 90 min). The majority of cross-country races in different age and performance groups can be completed between 30 and 120 minutes.

As well as very different course lengths, the course profiles can range greatly from almost flat to mountainous. Circuits with variations in altitude of several hundred meters are not unusual and place completely different demands on the cyclist than flat courses do.

Also, a course with sharp curves and enforced accelerations will have a very different requirement profile than a straighter course.

The great variety of these external performance factors allows for only a limited definition of the other performance factors.

Physical Conditioning

The mountain biker's metabolic state during a cross-country race mainly hovers around the aerobic-anaerobic threshold. The shorter the race, the greater the proportion of anaerobic metabolism (never more than 20% though) and, in a normal cross-country race, accounts for around 5% of the total race time. Anaerobic mobilization is particularly important during the often race-deciding start phase and also in intermediate attacks and in short climbs and accelerations coming out of tight curves.

Along with the metabolic status, the exercise heart rate in cross-country races, depending on motivation and race situation, is just below the anaerobic threshold with a few short peaks in the anaerobic area and occasionally a few short phases in the aerobic area (downhills). The racing heart rate of a well-trained biker with a maximum heart rate of about 200 bpm will be roughly 185 bpm. The metabolic status is therefore comparable to that of a road cycling time-trial on hilly terrain, although the heart rate does vary greatly as the effort required is constantly changing. In fact, the performance varies more than indicated by the heart rate values.

In training, therefore, the focus should be on improving aerobic capacity as much as possible without neglecting the anaerobic mobilization that plays such a key role.

Cross-country racing is also very demanding in terms of strength. The cross-country biker rides with a relatively low cadence (< 80 rpm) and uses a lot of power. Cadence progressions in a cross-country race alternate between rates of around 80 rpm and freewheeling phases. As well as excellent strength endurance to cope with the required gear ratios throughout the race, speed strength and maximum strength must both also be very well-developed to overcome very steep inclines both on the bike and on foot. If we take a look at the demand profile (SRM System) on page 136, the importance of strength endurance and speed strength in the many performance peaks on short climbs and accelerations is clear. So from the point of view of training methodology, speed strength must definitely be a priority. So, the size of the creatine phosphate stores is critical in determining performance capacity.

As can be seen in figure 3.29, cadence and power are constantly changing. It is a good idea to work on increasing the contractility of the pedaling muscles in training so as to be able to execute accelerations as economically as possible. The ability to repeat these short acceleration spurts frequently during a race (possibly several hundred times) is also vital.

At elite level, this is achieved by performing high numbers of repetitions in interval training.

The arm muscles play a greater role than in road cycling, which should be reflected in the training plan through strength training. The same is true for the core muscles; core strength must also be worked on in training.

Cross-country biking is also extremely demanding in terms of coordination, as riders must be able to master both tricky uphill sections and, like the downhillers, very difficult downhill sections. Many riders lose a lot of time on just these downhill or other demanding sections due to technical deficiencies—time that cannot be made up no matter how hard they try. This emphasizes the importance of technique training.

Mental Factors

Key mental factors include the concentration required often on demanding courses and strong motivation. Mental training should be part of the training program in order to develop these performance fundamentals.

Social Factors

Social performance factors include an optimal family and social environment (e.g., friends, club, team). Aim for a regular routine.

Cognitive Factors

The main cognitive challenges for the mountain biker are in the tactical area and in training planning and monitoring. Certain race situations require tactical mastery, although this is not usually a cognitive problem, that can only be learned from race experience. Although it is easy to recognize tactical errors once the race is over, it is equally easy to make poor decisions in a race during the heat of the moment.

Equipment Factors

Equipment is very important in mountain biking. It is especially important that equipment be adapted to the riding conditions (e.g., rough terrain) to avoid losing time. Adapting equipment to riding conditions also increases riding safety.

These factors, which only represent a rough overview, reveal the complexity of the performance structure in a very mentally and technically demanding sport like cross-country biking. There is no doubt that the cross-country biker must be extremely versatile and, to a great extent, must meet the demands of all the other mountain bike disciplines.

Compared to other cycling disciplines' performance structures, the greatest similarities are among cross-country cycling and short-circuit road racing (criteriums) and in points races or two-man tag racing on the track. These disciplines all feature spontaneous switches between intensive and less intensive phases. Particularly in criteriums, short laps must be negotiated at very high speeds. These disciplines also require well-developed anaerobic mobilization ability.

More detailed information on performance structure can be seen in chapter 3.9 in the charts prepared using the Schoberer (SRM) PowerMeter system.

2.2.2 Marathon

Marathons, unlike cross-country races, are long races on technically undemanding courses. Usually the race only involves completing one lap two or three times.

Race lengths at pro level can be up to four to five hours for both men and women. At grass-roots level, the starter can chose the race length himself, and marathons can last from two to twelve hours.

Aerobic capacity combined with well-developed strength endurance is the ideal foundation for successful marathon racing. The importance of anaerobic mobilization declines compared to the shorter races, although it is still required for the finishing spurt, for very steep climbs or intermediate attacks. The average heart rate is significantly lower than in cross-country races, but in the starting phase and in tactically critical situations, heart rate values can exceed the threshold.

The successful marathon biker is characterized by the ability to remain motivated over long distances and the ability to withstand pain.

Downhill: Peak concentration at high speed

Downhill qualities are also becoming more common for cross-country riders: World Cup in Dalby Forest, 2010 (UK).

2.2.3 Stage Races

Stage races are gaining popularity among mountain bikers, both at pro and grass-roots level, and they require other physiological factors in addition to the previously mentioned performance factors. The ability to recover quickly between stages is dependent on a well-trained aerobic capacity. Anaerobic mobilization becomes less important the longer the stage and tour, but is still important in the final sprint and in attacks.

If a mountain biker is unable to recover quickly due to neglecting recovery in special preparation and season planning, good performance is impossible because of problems in the aerobic and aerobic–anaerobic energy supplies and in strength, as the body is unable to regain the necessary energy capacity from one stage to the next.

The individual stages are very similar to the performance structure of a marathon, but the technical requirement is often slightly lower, although it can sometimes be really extreme, such as in some mountain pass crossings (e.g., the Trans Alp).

Motivation and commitment to the race are absolutely essential during a stage race.

Refreshments consumed during and after the race have a significant impact on the body's ability to recover and the next day's performance.

2.2.4 Downhills

Downhill races have different physical performance factor requirements than cross-country races. In comparatively short races lasting from a few minutes to occasionally more than 20 minutes, the importance of aerobic capacity declines. However, perfect coordination is vital as it must be constantly present, even when the heart rate is maximum. Therefore, a great deal of training time is spent on learning and perfecting technical riding skills.

Anaerobic capacity and strength are the main performance physiology requirements. The course, depending on its layout, may require frequent, short bursts of speed that draw on speed strength and maximum strength abilities. The performance structure is similar to that of 1000-meter racers and track sprinters and should be reflected in downhill training. Pedaling and other muscles are subject to short, sharp peak loads to cushion the shock from uneven surfaces and jumps.

Strength training for the arms and upper body should therefore be a regular part of the training program. A strong muscle corset protects the core in case of falls and also offers a certain performance reserve for extreme feats of strength.

Concentration, mental anticipation and fearlessness and pyschological features of the downhill performance structure. Mental training is necessary to visualize the course and to overcome fear.

Particularly in downhill, the right gear can make the difference between winning and losing a race. rapid Equipment that is obsolete or not adapted to the course conditions is a real handicap. Equipment is put under stain when pushed to the limit, and technical innovations that improve safety margins are directly transformed into faster performances.

Downhill races are now occasionally combined with enduro races, which are actually mainly composed of technical downhill races, but they also contain uphill sections. The Trail Trophy is a race concept which combines downhill, freeride and enduro race elements as well as uphill races and trial sections.

Speed strength plays a key role in 4-cross

2.2.5 4-Cross

The requirement profile of the brand new 4-cross discipline resembles that of downhill and dual slalom. As well as the requirements previously mentioned, the role of speed and strength is even more important, as the races are very short, lasting only between 60 and 120 seconds. Endurance takes a back seat, as in all downhill disciplines, but it cannot be completely neglected in 4-cross like in downhill because of the KO-race system and the fact that you race several times in one day. Excellent technical riding skills and the desire to prevail in direct rider contact are essential.

2.2.6 Dual Slalom

Dual slalom, like downhills and 4-cross, requires very good bike control. There is much less emphasis on aerobic capacity due to the short race duration. Fast accelerations are decisive, and training should be geared to outstanding speed strength and strength endurance. Strength training should not be so excessive that it negatively impacts coordination, though.

It is also crucial to have the right equipment.

2.2.7 Uphills

Uphill races are comparable to mountain time-trials or mountain races with mass starts. The race duration can range from a few minutes (mountain time-trials) in low mountain ranges up to more than one hour in the highlands. Uphill races are now quite rare and are usually only contested by cross-country bikers.

Excellent aerobic capacity and great strength are required to resist the downhill force. The low cadence and the fact that there is usually no opportunity for coasting in recovery phases mean that outstanding strength endurance is vital.

The shorter an uphill race, the more important the capacity for anaerobic mobilization, particularly at the end of the race. The heart rate values during a race lie at the anaerobic threshold and rise even higher at the end of the course.
Mountain time-trials require great mental toughness and motivation combined with excellent lactate tolerance.
Low cycling speeds lessen the importance of aerodynamics, although the weight of the mountain bike does have an impact.

2.2.8 Technical Races

Technical races comprise all kinds of trial races. As the name suggests, the focus is on the coordinated control of the mountain bike (trial bike). All other physical performance factors are secondary, although good basic fitness is also helpful in this technical discipline. Flexibility and strength (both speed and explosive strength) have the greatest influence on the performance structure.

Choosing the right equipment plays a key role here, too.

3

3   Training

3.1   Basic Principles of Training Theory

Training is a planned process, the aim of which is to improve or maintain athletic performance using appropriate training methods. Athletic performance not only includes pure, physical athletic ability, but also tactical, technical and mental aspects.

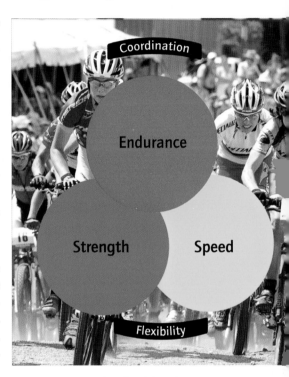

Fig 3.1: Basic Principles of Training Theory

The term conditioning includes five different basic abilities that are required in different proportions, depending on the sport. Basically, though, none of these elements should be overlooked in training.

From a biological point of view, training is the body's reaction to exercise. When the human body exercises, physical abilities improve, but if that exercise ceases, these abilities disappear (use it or lose it!). The correct training and rest sequence is crucial for training to be effective. Training disturbs the body's biological equilibrium so that after the rest phase the body adapts to the training load and achieves a higher performance level than before.

The following diagram illustrates the principle of supercompensation, one of the most important principles of training theory. Training stimulus, fatigue, recovery and supercompensation must occur in this order, with the correct time intervals between them. Recovery is the process by which the body recuperates from fatigue and lasts until the previous performance level has been regained. Supercompensation is performance improvement following recovery; it is a kind of "over-recovery". The improved performance level is reached because the recovery does not stop when the previous performance level has been reached. Recovery continues until a performance level that can maintain the same training load on the next occasion has been reached. This process is known as **adaptation**.

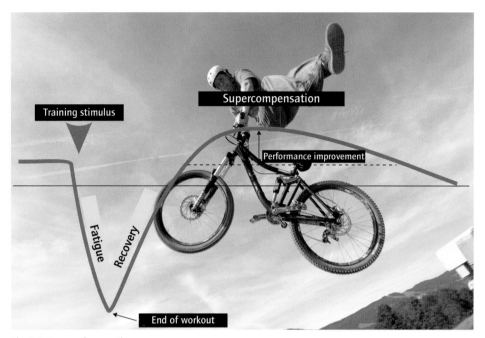

Fig. 3.2: Supercompensation

Once a high training level has been reached, improvements in performance level become less and less until eventually reaching a performance-level plateau.

This is why very fit mountain bikers need very high training volumes and sophisticated training plans to maintain or, if possible, improve their performance level. Maximum training loads, well-planned and performed for many years, are essential for success at international level. In the cross-country World Cup, the level is so high that there can no longer be surprise winners (complete unknowns), who had not previously competed at international level in a related sport (road, cross-country). You can read more on physiological adaptation processes in chapter 2.1

In the **adaptation** process, metabolic adaptation is limited by morphological adaptation (physical adaptation, e.g., muscles, heart). Mountain bike training leads to significant adaptation processes, both metabolic and morphological, as described in more detail in chapter 2.1, From Beginner to Pro From a Physiological Perspective.

Fig. 3.3: Performance
development over many
years of endurance trai-
ning with increasing
training workload
(diagram)

Time

3.1.1 Description of Training Load

Training intensity

means the extent of the workload from a loading stimulus or training session. The easiest way to establish training intensity in mountain biking is by measuring heart rate (high intensity = high heart rate). Other intensity indicators are lactate concentration or speed.

Training volume

is the total of all loading or training stimuli performed per training session or trai- ning period (e.g., week, preparation phase). In mountain biking, training volume can be compared to training mileage or, better still, by the training duration (e.g., 22 hrs/wk or 6 hrs basic training); training sessions without the bike (gym trai- ning, exercises, running training, strength training) should also be included when calculating training volume.

Loading concentration

gives the relationship between loading and rest (recovery) and the rest duration between the individual training stimuli, while differentiating between complete and incomplete rest. Complete rest means waiting until the body has completely recovered before resuming training. This again can be measured by heart rate or by how your body feels. Incomplete rest is over when the heart rate returns to levels of 120–130 bpm, at which point training is resumed.

Loading duration

is the length of a bout of training, such as an interval (three minutes) or a series of sprints (6 x 20 sec).

Training frequency

means how often per week training takes place.

These five basic training factors are accurate parts of the training process and are used repeatedly below.

If training workloads are set correctly, the performance level will improve up to an individual performance limit, which in an endurance sport like mountain biking can only be achieved after many years of training. It is therefore impossible to attain elite performances after a year training, especially if no other endurance sports have been practiced previously. This fact is often hard to understand and a source of frustration for those new to mountain biking.

The following graph shows a training sequence that is too short; training resumes before the recovery process is over, making it impossible for the performance level to improve and instead causing it to dip.

Performance stagnation would be the result of training too infrequently (i.e., when training is resumed only after the supercompensation is over, when the condition of the body is almost the same as before training). This results in little or no training progress. Figure 3.4 shows that training must resume right in the middle (high point) of the supercompensation phase for optimal performance improvement. As well as the recovery lengths between the training sessions, the training and racing themselves must be right for performance to improve; more on this in the next chapter. If the training workload is too low, the adaptation process will not be triggered, while too much training, in the long term, leads to overtraining. Only the correct training will cause the desired adaptation and supercompensation. Correct training means that training type, volume and intensity, and the rest phases must all be perfectly aligned.

When deciding on rest phases and drawing up a training plan, awareness of your own body is also important. Suggested training plans, like those in this book, must be adapted to individual circumstances. A training plan should not be viewed as being set in stone.

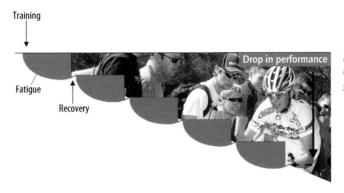

Fig. 3.4:
Correct and incorrect
sequencing of training

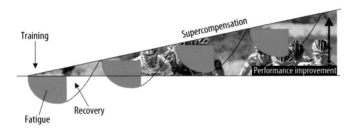

3.1.2   Recovery

If all that was required to be successful was to train very hard every day, a whole raft of mountain bikers would probably be performing at a much higher level. Recovery is just as important as training and is an essential and integral part of a good training plan. Next we examine how to determine the correct relationship between loading and recovery.

What determines the duration of the recovery phase?
A simple basic principle of recovery states that the harder or more exhausting the training or race, the longer the body will take to recover, because the body needs longer to compensate for the disruption, or biological imbalance caused to its tissues.

Illnesses like infections or inflammations usually have a negative impact on recovery. Daily workouts then become more demanding, and the recovery phase takes longer. After heavy head colds, recovery can be affected for two to three weeks, significantly affecting performance levels.

"No pain, No gain"

How is recovery affected?
Recovery is only affected when post-training and racing preconditions are optimal, but there is no "miracle method" that enables immediate recovery. Particularly during periods of intensive training and racing, for example at training camps or at race weekends, recovery should not be left to chance but should be actively supported.

Factors that enhance recovery:
- Sufficient rest (sleep)
- Recovery nutrition
- Stretching
- Massage
- Warm bath or shower
- Sauna
- Active recovery (walking)
- Relaxation techniques and recovery training

Sufficient rest means not only avoiding unnecessary effort after exercise, but also includes getting sufficient bed rest. **Nutrition** must be very high in carbohydrates, vitamins and minerals in order to replenish the empty energy reserves (see chapter 7, Nutrition). **Stretching** lowers muscle tone, gently stimulates the metabolism, maintains flexibility and should be performed daily.

A **recovery massage** reduces muscle tone, accelerates the elimination of metabolites and, above all, promotes relaxation. A **warm bath** lasting about 15 minutes lowers muscle tone, stimulates the metabolism, relaxes and rests the body. **Relaxation techniques** are described in more detail in chapter 9.

Recovery training on the bike (CT, see chapter 3.2) is a good way of speeding up the elimination of metabolites from the muscles and is the most important method of active recovery, along with walking, which has a similar effect.

Endurance training significantly enhances recovery ability. After an exhausting race, very well-trained mountain bikers are usually fresh and recovered just a few minutes after crossing the finish line, while novices find it hard to recover at all from a mountain section, for example, and may even have to drop out of the race or training session.

Phase	Recovery process	Comments
Early phase **Up to 6 hrs after exercise**	• Refilling CP and ATP reserves • Eliminating blood lactate • Start refilling glycogen reserves • Normalizing heart and breathing rates	Important phase for glycogen resynthesis; essential to consume sufficient carbohydrates and fluids. Note: increased danger of infection when cooling off and overtraining.
Late phase About 6–36 hrs after exercise	• Refilling glycogen reserves • Regenerating protein structures (mitochondria) • Recovering immune defense completely	Continued sufficient carbohydrate intake, plus different recovery measures, especially compensatory training (30 min) and stretching
Supercompensation **About 36 hrs to several** **weeks after exercise**	• Balancing electrolyte and possible supercompensation • Reestablishing hormone balance • Supercompensation of structural proteins • Supercompensation in hormone and enzyme balances	Supercompensation, especially in protein structures, can take several weeks (e.g., after a training camp or a stage race). This must be taken into consideration in training.

Fig. 3.5: Duration of different recovery processes

What does recovery feel like?

As described, recovery is an individual process which can vary from one rider to another even after the same amount of exercise. Age also affects recovery duration, as well as the previously-mentioned factors. Young bikers recover faster than older ones with similar fitness levels. Bikers with many years of training experience (high training age) also recover more quickly, and women recover more quickly than men.

The way your body feels during training and racing is the most accurate source of feedback regarding your recovery. Other indications of a completed recovery are a positive attitude, the desire to train and achieve, good sleep, a good appetite, normal resting and training heart rate and the feeling of being healthy. The lack of one or more of these factors indicate that recovery is not yet complete. The aim of the "self-coaching mountain biker" should be to establish his own recovery requirements following different types and amounts of exercise.

High-Tech Recovery

The previous methods are complemented by modern sports medicine techniques. These techniques are able to determine endurance athletes' recovery states accurately by using various blood parameters.

This is done by testing for concentrations of different minerals and creatine kinase, urea and other metabolites in the blood. In addition, an immunological evaluation of recovery using the determination of cell counts and the activity of different immune cells is also possible.

This science is still in its infancy, and bigger research projects into recovery have only been initiated in recent years, the results of which are likely to be the first steps toward recovery-based training management.

However, it is still possible to evaluate recovery even at elite level simply using a little experience and the traditional methods previously mentioned.

Acrobatic stunt by Miguel Martinez, Spa 2005

3.1.3 Mountain Bike Training Principles

Training principles address the physiological effects of training as well as the body's adaptation processes to exercise and are the foundation of training planning.

Principle of Effective Training

This principle states that training must be of a sufficient intensity in order to produce a training effect. The degree of this intensity in endurance training is dependent on the athlete's fitness and how the athlete feels on the day. For example, an endurance mountain bike ride of 30 minutes a day with a heart rate of 110 bpm would not cause a training effect in an experienced cyclist and would only be useful as a recovery workout, whereas it may represent a high training workload for a rehabilitation patient.

Principle of Progressive Overload

In order to achieve the long-term goal of performance improvement, training and racing loads must be appropriate for the fitness level. As fitness levels increase, the training workload must also increase in order to improve or even just maintain form. This increase should be even and gradual. However, at elite level, this is no longer enough to produce a training effect, and the workload must be increased abruptly in order to trigger adaptations.

Principle of Loading Variation

Like the progressive overload, loading during the year must not only be increased but also varied. This is particularly true for elite-level mountain bikers, who must use completely new training methods (e.g., cross-training) in order to be able to break through performance barriers caused by monotonous training.

Principle of Optimal Sequencing of Exercise and Recovery

This principle is already explained in detail in sections 3.1 and 3.2. Supercompensation and recovery are critical factors in sports training.

Principle of Periodization and Cyclization

As a mountain biker cannot maintain peak form for a whole season, the training year must be divided into phases with different types of training to ensure that peak performances are achieved at the desired time. Chapter 3.5 addresses this topic in detail.

Principle of Individuality and Age-Appropriateness

Individual mountain bikers must train differently due to their different biological make-ups. A biker's training plan must also take into account their personal circumstances and abilities. For youngsters, age is an important factor when it comes to the selection of training activity, while for adults, training age is important.

Principle of Increasing Specialization

In the course of a training year, and even during a mountain biking career, the importance of specific training methods increases. For example, if the athlete is still doing a great deal of cross-training at the start of the year, during the season the focus is more on actual bike training. Likewise, the proportion of actual bike training constantly increases from low levels for youngsters in basic training to very high levels for World Cup competitors in peak performance training.

Principle of Training Awareness

The principle of training awareness is vital, as it encourages the athlete to think about training content. Before a training session, the biker should be completely clear about the goal of the session and what should and should not be done in order to achieve this goal. However, too often, training is performed without any real awareness of its actual training goal. This principle is particularly relevant for coaches.

3.1.4 Training Methodology

Endurance

Endurance, in general, is the body's increased ability to withstand fatigue and the resulting recovery (resistance to fatigue, both physical and mental).

There are several different forms of endurance training.
Local endurance is the opposite of general endurance; local endurance applies to less than 1/6 of all muscles. In cycling, the use of large muscle groups (the legs) corresponds to *general endurance.* Depending on the type of metabolism involved, we distinguish between aerobic and anaerobic endurance; in mountain biking, both aerobic and anaerobic endurance are required. There is yet another difference between *static endurance* (without movement) and *dynamic endurance* (movement).

Figure 3.6 shows approximate values for the respective loading durations. The heart rates are based on a maximum heart rate of about 210 bpm. Only the most important performance-limiting factors are provided.

Downhill racing only falls into this endurance category if an almost constant, maximum pedaling action is required. Very technically demanding courses with only short, intensive pedaling phases are hard to classify and are categorized according to the sum of the pedaling phases and their chronological order.

1) Endurance Training Methodology
The **endurance training** method is mainly used to build up basic endurance.

    a. Continuous method: Constant intensity; heart rate measurement is the most accurate way of monitoring effort. The continuous endurance training method is

	STE	MTE	LTE I	LTE II	LTE III	LTE IV
Duration	35 s – 2 min	2 min – 10 min	10 min – 35 min	35 min – 90 min	90 min – 6 h	> 6 h
MTB race type	(Downhill) Uphill sprints	Downhill Uphill	(Downhill) Uphill Cross-Country	(Uphill) Cross-Country	Marathon Cross-Country	Marathon
HF/min	185 – 200	190 – 210	180 – 190	170 – 190	150 – 180	120 – 170
% VO$_2$max	100	95 – 100	90 – 95	80 – 95	60 – 90	50 – 60
Aerobic %	20 – 35	40 – 60	70 – 80	80 – 90	95	99
Anaerobic &	80 – 65	60 – 40	30 – 20	20 – 10	5	1
Energy source	Glycogen	Glycogen	Glycogen	Glycogen	Fat, glycogen	Fat, glycogen
Main substrate	Phosphate			Fat	Amino acids	Amino acids
Limiting factors	High speed and strength	High aerobic and anaerobic capacity	Anaerobic threshold	Anaerobic threshold	Anaerobic threshold	Lipolysis
			VO$_2$max	VO$_2$max	VO$_2$max	Water balance
	Aerobic ability	High speed and strength	Acidity tolerance	Glycogen reserves	Glycogen reserves	Carbohydrate intake
	Coordination (technique)	High acidity tolerance	Lactic acid elimination		Water balance	
				Thermo-regulation		
	High acidity-tolerance	VO$_2$max-coordination			Lipolysis	

Fig. 3.6: Endurance types, differentiated according to loading duration (modified after Neumann & Berbalk; STE = short-term endurance, MTE = medium-term endurance, LTE = long-term endurance)

the most frequently used training method in mountain biking, especially in the preparation phase, as at the appropriate intensity it improves aerobic capacity and recovery ability. Training should last at least two, possibly up to five to eight hours. The training intensity can either be constant or vary within a narrow range.

b. *Alternate method:* Over previously determined course sections; the tempo is raised until the aerobic-anaerobic mixed zone.

c. *Fartlek:* Tthe tempo is adapted to the terrain and wind conditions. The biker plays with tempo and also with intensity. Fartlek is mainly used over hilly terrain or in the woods.

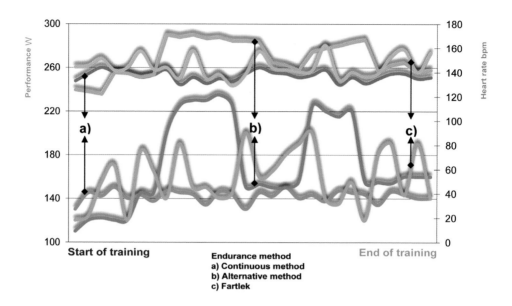

Fig. 3.7: Graph representing the continuous, alternate and fartlek methods

2) The interval method

The **interval method** involves the systematic alternating of exercise and rest, in which the rest interval is not long enough to allow for complete recovery, but a new interval is started once the heart rate drops to about 120–140 bpm (i.e., "just enough" recovery). The interval method is used in sprint training (e.g., 8 x 7 sec or 6 x 30 sec). If several series are performed, there should be a longer rest between the individual series of 4–8 reps. The rest length is about 1–2 minutes for short sprints (speed strength training) and for long intervals of 4,000 meters it should be about 5–10 minutes depending on performance level. The rest breaks are active but very low intensity (e.g., slow walking at an easy pace in the CT zone).

The different types of interval training are grouped according to interval length:

a. Short interval (SI): 7–60 seconds (e.g., 10 x 7 sec, 6 x 30 sec)
b. Medium interval (MI): 1–3 minutes (e.g., 4 x 1:30 min)
c. Long interval (LI): 3–15 minutes (e.g., 4 x 10 min)

The short interval method is also known as the intensive interval method, and the long interval method is also the extensive interval method; medium intervals can belong to either method depending on the intensity.

The extensive interval method serves to raise the anaerobic threshold and to improve aerobic capacity and anaerobic mobilization. The intensive interval method improves lactate tolerance, raises the anaerobic lactic acid and anaerobic alactic acid capacity (see chapter 2), improves the ability to recover from short, steep climbs and enhances speed and speed strength.

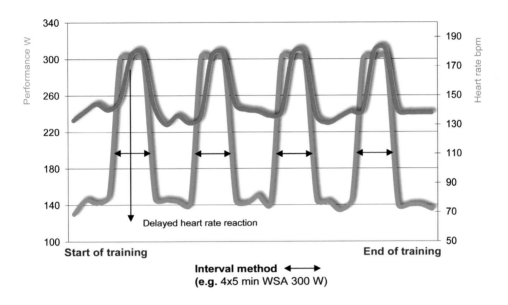

Fig. 3.8: Graph of the interval method ("just enough" recovery)

3) Repetition Method

The **repetition method** is characterized by complete recovery rest breaks (heart rate below 100 bpm) between intervals ridden at or above race intensity. This method is not commonly used in cross-country biking but is very common in track cycling (e.g., sessions of 3 x 1000 m). In cross-country, the repetition method allows a strength training session to be carried out in the mountains, involving about two to three minutes of maximum exercise followed by a rest phase that is initially active and then passive, until the heart rate has dropped back below 90 bpm. The repetition method is likewise subdivided into short, medium and long. The repetition method is used particularly often in downhill, with the execution of maximum speed pedaling intervals.

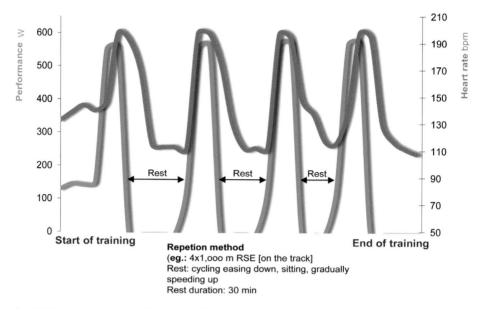

Fig. 3.9: Graph showing repetition method (complete rest to full recovery)

4) Racing and Monitoring Methods

These methods involve a one-off effort at race intensity and duration.

The physiological training load is very similar to that of a typical race in terms of course length and speed In over-distance training (when the training distance is longer than the race distance), the effort/intensity should be slightly below race intensity, and in under-distance training it should slightly exceed it. These methods require considerable motivation in order to be able to emulate a race performance. Unorganized training races around a circuit are ideal, as they simulate the physical, technical, tactical and mental aspects of actual races. The race method should, however, only be used at the end of the preparation phase or even just at the start of the competition phase. For the purposes of performance monitoring (monitoring method) and simple performance testing, time-trials or uphills are suitable.

The racing method provides an opportunity to practice tactics and improve mental racing toughness. Note that it is important to train in a training group where all riders have similar abilities.

Strength

Strength is the basic physical quality that allows us to move; without a certain amount of strength, movement is impossible. A description of the different types of muscle contraction can be found in chapter 2.

The different types of strength are described only briefly next. Sport science has traditionally identified three main types of strength, along with many subforms. Although more recent research has identified other types, the traditional model is used for the sake of simplicity. The explanation in chapter 2 of how the muscles work is very important for strength training.

a. *Maximum Strength*

Maximum strength refers to the strength an athlete can exert voluntarily during maximum muscular contraction. According to recent discoveries, maximum strength plays a more important role than had previously been thought as the foundation of all other types of strength, even for mountain biking.

b. *Speed Strength*

Speed strength is the athlete's ability to overcome resistance with fast muscle contraction speed and is highly influenced by the level of maximum strength. Speed strength is important in cross-country, where it is particularly needed for steep climbs, sprints, attacks and overcoming obstacles and jumps.

c. *Strength Endurance*

Strength endurance is the ability to withstand fatigue over frequently-repeated strength loads. Strength endurance is defined as about 30–50% of maximum strength, performed dynamically, and is vital in uphill sections and breakaway attempts requiring high to maximum gear ratios combined with high effort. This can be shown by a simple equation in which strength and cadence are proportional: the higher the cadence at a constant speed, the lower the strength input; the lower the cadence at a constant speed, the higher the strength input. Cadences are relatively low in mountain biking.

Strength Training Methodology

In strength training, training content is described in terms of reps and sets; one set can consist of up to 20 or more reps, performed consecutively without a break, although there is a recovery break between the sets.

The topic of strength training methodology is addressed in detail in chapter 4.

Cape Eric in South Africa—one of the toughest stage races for bikers

Speed

Speed is defined as the ability of the muscles to contract as fast as possible. There are two types of speed: the speed of a single movement (movement speed, cadence) and speed of locomotion (riding speed). Movements may either be cyclical or acyclical. An example of acyclical speed is shot-putting or javelin throwing.

Cycling involves a constantly repeated (i.e., cyclical) motion, which is why cyclical speed is so important for mountain bikers. Cyclical speed (movement speed) depends on the gear ratio used: If the gear ratio is high, the cadence and the movement speed will be low, although forward motion speed may be very high. A combination of high cadence and really high strength input sustained for a long period of time (high gear ratio, strength endurance) results in very fast cycling speeds. This shows how dependent speed is on strength; it is impossible to reach sustained high velocities without an appropriately high level of strength. Training should therefore focus on improving both speed and strength.

Speed training is less important in cross-country racing but is essential in downhill and slalom where fast muscle speed is needed for short, maximum accelerations and is a key performance factor.

Speed Training Methodology

Speed training is done using the repetition method performed at high intensities and with movement sequences that are as cycling-specific as possible (on the mountain bike or racing bike). The workout duration should reflect racing requirements (short accelerations of 6–8 sec and longer pedaling sections in the downhill up to 40 sec). Speed training is most effective when performed in blocks on consecutive days.

For speed training, see also Speed Training in chapter 3.2.

Flexibility

Flexibility is the ability to perform a movement with the largest possible range of motion. Good flexibility is an essential prerequisite for good movement technique.

The main problem of poor flexibility is that it means an increased susceptibility to injury. For example, if in a fall the joints and ligaments lack sufficient range of motion, a ligament or a tendon can be torn or even snapped much more easily, and even bone fractures are more common. Poor flexibility hinders the development of conditioning and coordination. Flexibility enables a more economical cycling action and promotes recovery, and, especially in the technical disciplines and in the downhill, it is a basic prerequisite for good bike control.

Flexibility is largely dependent on the elasticity of the muscles, which is why I have devoted a whole chapter to it (chapter 5).

Flexibility Training Methodology

You should aim for very good mountain-bike-specific and adequate general flexibility. Once optimal flexibility has been attained, you must keep it up otherwise it can very quickly revert to the starting level. Choose exercises that are appropriate for the race or training-specific activity, and perform them either during the warm-up or cool-down phases of the workout. Training should definitely be performed daily at elite level.

For more information on how to improve flexibility, see chapter 5 Functional Stretching.

Coordination

Coordination is the athlete's ability to exert maximum effort with minimal and targeted muscle effort.

Mountain biking in general and downhill in particular require a great deal of cycling-specific coordination, while the general coordination of the mountain biker is not usually very well developed. Very often, at the start of a "career," coordination and flexibility training are completely neglected, and this gap is never really filled. However, cycling-specific coordination may be excellent; for example, the round pedaling action, jumps, starts, curve riding and standing are indications of very highly developed coordination skills. In order to counteract a loss of general coordination due to incorrect pedaling, starting from a young age, general coordination should be developed (e.g., training indoors in winter). Chapter 8, Technique Training, explores ways of improving coordination in more detail.

Coordination Training Methodology

Coordination and cycling technique are closely linked, which is why many coordination training tips can be found in the technique section. Coordination training without a bike takes place indoors in winter but should also be continued throughout the season.

Coordination training should always be performed when the body is fresh, not at the end of a tough workout when coordination would be reduced. A workout to develop the round pedaling action could, for example, be combined with a compensatory/recovery session. Cycling technique practice, such as clearing obstacles, touching the rear wheel of the rider in front with your own front wheel or other tricks and stunts can be performed on a rest day (training camp).

It is important not to neglect general coordination in your haste to improve your cycling-specific coordination, as it facilitates the learning of new skills on the bike.

3.2   Training Zones

Training is divided into zones to facilitate planning. The zones group exercise according to its intensity and type.

Training zones derived from metabolic processes.
Training zones based on the metabolic processes described in chapter 2 that specifically correspond to and train each different metabolism.

The three main metabolic areas are:
  •   Aerobic
  •   Aerobic–anaerobic mixed
  •   Anaerobic

Compensatory training and basic endurance training 1 are classified as aerobic training. Basic endurance 2, strength endurance and race-specific endurance training correspond to the aerobic–anaerobic mixed zone. Anaerobic lactic acid zone is covered by speed training and the training of race-specific endurance, while the alactic acid zone is covered by speed strength training.

The terms chosen for each training zone are those used mainly in endurance training theory, like **compensatory training, basic endurance 1 and 2, strength endurance and race-specific endurance**. Because of the similarities with road cycling, there are no new terms for mountain biking.

Basic endurance 2 corresponds to what in the cycling literature is usually called development training; race-specific endurance has many similarities with elite training.

Compensatory Training (CT)

Compensatory training (CT) involves helping the body to recovery from exercise or a recovery deficit by active, sport-specific recovery. CT training intensity is the lowest of all training types.

Compensatory Training	
Description	Recovery training to regain performance ability after intensive training and racing and to warm-up before and cool-down after exercise
Heart rate	80-120 bpm
Metabolism	Purely aerobic, lipolysis Lactic acid below 2.0 mmol/l Training example CT (e.g., 60 min CT with 39 x 18)
Duration	0:30-2:00 h
Volume (road)	15-50 km
Cadence	70-100 U/min
Gear ratio	4.6-6.0 m
Methods	Endurance method
Periodization	Used throughout the year, but less so in PP I and II, an important component of the microcycle in the competition phase
Cyclization	Especially after intensive races and workouts: usually on Mondays and before a race
Organization type	Individual and group training
Course/terrain	On the road, if possible
Mountain bike/ Racing bike	With slicks on the MTB or on the racing bike
Tips	Put as little pressure as possible on the pedals, dress warmly and technique can be incorporated into CT training.

Fig. 3.10: Compensatory training (PP: preparation phase, CP: competition phase)

Basic Endurance Training (BE)

The most important intensity and training zone in mountain biking is the aerobic metabolism. This area is also called basic endurance. A very high percentage (about 60–75%) of the total annual training volume is performed in this zone in order to hinder lactate production. An excellent basic endurance foundation is essential to be able to cope with high racing loads in the aerobic or mixed metabolic zones.

In keep-fit mountain biking, more than 90% of total training volume is performed in the basic endurance zone. Most cross-training without a bike is also performed in this zone.

Basic endurance training workouts feature high to very high volumes and low intensities. The basic endurance zone is further divided into two intensity levels: basic endurance 1 and basic endurance 2.

Basic Endurance 1 (BE 1)

In workouts lasting from two to over seven hours (with the road bike 60 to over 200 km), the energy supply is exclusively aerobic with a high fat-burning element. This training zone is excellent for fat burning and is the most beneficial from a health point of view (overweight). Slick tires on the mountain bike should be used in this zone.

Basic Endurance 2 (BE2)

The BE 2 trains the lower regions of the aerobic–anaerobic transition zone, with a distinction made between strength and cadence-oriented training. The following section deals with the individual heart rate in the training zones. It is a good idea to incorporate BE 2 intervals into a BE 1 workout. A long (over 3 hours) training ride performed exclusively in the BE 2 area is very exhausting and empties the glycogen reserves, which is desirable during carbohydrate loading, for example (see chapter 7, Nutrition). In total, the BE 2 zone accounts for only about 5% of the total training volume.

Race-Specific Endurance (RSE)

Training in the RSE area is geared, as the name suggests, to competition speed and effort and is situated in the upper aerobic–anaerobic mixed zone. Depending on individual fitness levels, it is performed at or above race-pace. Training in the race-specific zone can either be performed with very high cadence and low power effort, with racing cadence and race gear ratio, or with high gear ratios, appropriately low cadences and high strength input. In RSE training with the mountain bike on hilly terrain, the exercise intensity often fluctuates wildly due to the course profile.

Basic Endurance Training 1 (BE1)

Description	Important training zone for mountain bikers in order to create a high aerobic capacity as the foundation of a high performance level and to warm-up before training or racing
Heart Rate	115–145 bpm
Metabolism	Purely aerobic, lipolysis Duration Lactic acid 0–2.5 (3.0) mmol/l 2–8 hrs
Training example	BE1: 4 hrs BE1 with 39 x 16 on the flat, suitable gear ratios on hilly terrain
Volume (road)	50–250 km/31– 155 mi
Cadence	80–110 rpm Ideally 100 U/min
Gear ratio	4.7–6.4 m (e.g., 42 x 19 – 14 [racing bike])
Methods	Endurance methods
Periodization	Used throughout the year, particularly important in the preparation phase, stick to aerobic zone BE 1 in all other cross-training sports in the PPs; it is an essential element of a spring training camp.
Cyclization	Train in blocks as much as possible: 3:1, 4:1 or 5:1 (e.g., 3 hrs, 4 hrs, 5 hrs, 1 hrs) CT during the competition phase ideally from Tuesday to Thursday if weekends are race-free, or in the preparation phase from Friday to Sunday.
Organization form	Training alone is best, monitor intensity via heart rate Change leader frequently in group training in order to maintain constant intensity (1–2 min)
Course/Terrain	Where possible on the road or on smooth paths, flat to undulating
Mountain bike/ Racing bike	With slicks on the MTB or on the racing bike
Tips	Try to determine individual heart rate values by performance testing; if possible do not train above 150 bpm, a range of about 20 bpm is optimal. Speed is not a monitoring parameter.

Fig. 3.11: Basic endurance training 1 (PP: preparation phase; CP: competition phase)

Basic Endurance 2 (BE2)

Description	Medium-intensity training zone to build up race-specific endurance and raise the anaerobic threshold, improve lactate elimination and optimize the aerobic–anaerobic transition; strength or motor skills training possible depending on the desired goal; in strength-oriented BE 2—train with high gears and low cadence
Heart rate	About 145–175 bpm
Metabolism	Aerobic–anaerobic transition Duration Lactic acid 3.0–6.0 mmol/l 0.15–2 hrs
Training example	BE 2: 4 x 20 min BE 2 in 3 hrs BE 1 training
Volume (road)	5–70 km/3–43.5 miles, flat to undulating
Cadence	100–120 rpm, 70–95 rpm
Gear ratio	5.6–7.6 m (e.g., 42 x 16-52 x 15)
Methods	Interval methods
Periodization	In the PP II and II and particularly in the CP, although the longer the race, the less BE 2 training is carried out
Cyclization	During the CP, on Wednesdays or also Thursdays, advisable as well as a short BE 2 course the day before a race
Organization	Training alone: self-motivation not easy, monitor intensity via heart rate and cadence Group training: frequent change of leader in order to maintain constant intensity (1–2 min)
Course/Terrain	Also possible in off-road paths, flat to undulating, or on longer mountains
Mountain bike/ Racing bike	With slicks or fat treads on the MTB, racing bike
Tips	Important to establish individual heart rate values using performance testing, range of 10–15 beats is optimal, speed is not a monitoring parameter, use for pre-race warm-up, the volume relates to the whole BE 2 distance covered

Fig. 3.12: Basic endurance training 2 (PP: preparation phase; CP: competition phase)

Race-Specific Endurance (RSE)

Description	High-intensity training zone to improve stamina, lactate tolerance and elimination; development of the feeling for pace; races can also be used as workouts; time-trials over different distances are very important
Heart rate	About 170–185 bpm
Metabolism	Aerobic/anaerobic metabolism Lactic acid above 5.0 mmol/l — Duration 0.04 – 1:30 hrs
Training example	4 x 6 min with 53 x 15 or 2 x 25 min with 53 x 16
Volume (road)	50 km/31 mi, flat to hilly (road)
Cadence	80–120 rpm, ideally 100 rpm
Gear	6.2–9.2 m (e.g., 52 x 18-52 x 12 [racing bike])
Methods	Interval methods, repetition method, competition method
Periodization	In the PP II and CP, particularly important in race preparation
Cyclization	During the CP, on Wednesdays or also Thursdays advisable (only rarely, as very intensive)
Organization	Training alone: as time-trial training, monitor intensity by heart rate Group training: as team time-trial training
Course/Terrain	Both on- and off-road, if possible On undulating courses strive for constant effort during the intervals
Mountain bike/ Racing bike	Both mountain and racing bikes
Tips	Try to determine individual heart rate values via performance testing; range of about 20 beats is optimal; speed is not a monitoring parameter; perform technically demanding training races and time-trials

Fig. 3.13: Race-specific endurance (PP: preparation phase; CP: competition phase)

Special Training Zones

The special training zones account for only a small percentage of the total training and, unlike the previously mentioned zones, heart rate is not the main method for monitoring intensity. Instead, they involve executing a specific movement sequence, which, depending on performance level, leads to different levels of difficulty with different physiological loading parameters.

Strength Endurance Training (SE)

The aim of strength endurance training is to improve the ability to withstand fatigue when performing high, cyclically repeating strength loads. In order to be able to train with increased resistance, the training rides should be performed on a mountain or pass with a gentle incline. With a high gear ratio, the relatively flat incline is tackled with a cadence between 40 and 60 rpm per minute in the seated position. This is an excellent way of training the round pedaling action, particularly the pull phase.

Strength training has gained importance in recent years, for higher and higher speeds are attempted, especially with greater gear ratios. The high strength load and low movement frequency ensure that the intensity remains in the aerobic-anaerobic transition zone.

If the heart rate reaches maximum levels, it means that the strength load is too low and the cadence too high, and a higher gear ratio must be used.

A good way of developing race-specific strength endurance is to ride a mountain course of at least 4-kilometers (2.5 mi) long with racing gear ratios, including simulations of several (3–5) breakaway attempts over 300 meters (330 yds), in which the gear ratio is increased. End with a finishing sprint over the last 500 meters (550 yds). This method should only be used rarely as it is very intensive.

If you do not have access to mountains on which to perform SE training, a flat course can also be used. If possible, the flat course needs a strong, constant headwind, although this is still a compromise. When this training is done on the flat and at elite level, use the highest gear ratios on the racing bike (e.g., 53 x 12). Because of the high strength load, this method can cause blood pressure spikes, making this type of strength training inappropriate for keep-fit cyclists.

Speed Training (ST)

Speed training is one of the special training zones and is not the same as speed strength training. Speed here does not mean cycling speed, but movement speed, which in mountain biking means cadence. Both pure speed and speed endurance are trained. Even though the cadences used in mountain biking are relatively low, speed training to improve movement economy is still necessary.

Strength Endurance Training (SE)	
Description	Medium-intensity training zone specifically to improve strength endurance; at low cadences inclines are ridden in the saddle with high gear ratios
Heart rate	About 145–175 bpm
Metabolism	Aerobic–anaerobic metabolism Duration Lactic acid 3-5 mmol/l 0:20–1:30 hrs
Training example	1 x 20 km SE; gear ratio important: warm-up and cool-down; if no long mountain course is handy, ride a short mountain course several times, or long distances (30 km/18.5 mi) into a strong headwind
Cadence	40–60 rpm
Volume (road)	3–30 km/2–18.5 mi
Gear ratio	5.2–8.0 m (racing bike) (e.g., 52 x 21 – 52 x 14)
Methods	Repetition method, usually not more than three reps
Periodization	Important in PP I, II and II and in the CP, particularly in cross-country and downhill. In PP I, if done at all, SE should only be trained on the flat
Cyclization	Train in blocks during CP on Wednesdays or Thursdays
Organization	Train alone Group training: improves motivation; problem: do not race in the mountains
Course/Terrain	Both off-road (not on rough tracks) and on the road; hilly stretches are particularly suitable, although they must enable constant effort
Mountain bike/ Racing bike	Both mountain bike and racing bike
Tips	Ride uphill in the saddle; sit as still as possible; deliberate pedaling action (pull); start off in easy gears; speed is not a monitoring parameter; perform regularly; stop if having joint problems; and, when pain-free, build up slowly (i.e., slowly increase loading)

Fig. 3.14: Strength endurance training (PP: preparation period; CP: competition period)

Speed Training (ST)

Description	High-intensity training zone above the anaerobic threshold to improve speed and speed endurance as well as lactate tolerance and stamina
Heart rate	Toward the end of the load, above anaerobic threshold Đ 175 bpm
Metabolism	Anaerobic or mixed metabolism $\qquad$ Duration Lactate above 6.0 mmol/l depending on duration $\quad$ 0:40–8:00 min
Training example	3 x 1 km ST interspersed with CT/BE 1 sections, gear ratio (e.g., 42 x 16 or 3 x 1 min), important to warm up and cool down
Cadence	120–max rpm
Volume (profile)	0.5–5 km, flat
Gear ratio	5.2–7.5 m (e.g., 42 x 17–52 x 15 [racing bike])
Methods	Interval method (short to long intervals)
Periodization	In the PP I and II at the end of each phase and in the CP, particularly important in the preparation for downhills and short cross-country races
Cyclization	During the CP, on Tuesdays or also advisable on Wednesdays (only rarely, as very intensive)
Organization forms	Individual training: intensity monitoring by cadence Group training: improves motivation, easier to maintain high cadence
Course/Terrain	Both on- and off-road On slightly downhill courses or with a following wind to increase cadence
Mountain bike/ Racing bike	Both mountain bike and racing bike
Tips	Speed is not a monitoring parameter, perform regularly Performance monitoring: maximum cadence test

Fig. 3.15: Speed training (PP: preparation phase; CP: competition phase)

Speed Strength Training (SS)

Description	Specific, high-intensity training zone to improve speed and maximum strength Improvement of the anaerobic alactic metabolism; in the case of short rests, also lactic acid component, the figures for short rests are given in brackets
Heart rate	Not relevant Duration 6–12 x 6 – 8 sec, 1–3 sets
Metabolism	Anaerobic alactic, lactate < 2.5 (4.0) mmol/l
Training Example	3 x 1,000 m ST interspersed with CT/BE 1 sections; gear ratio (e.g., 52 x 15); rest length 1–2 min, important to warm up and cool down
Volume (profile)	Include in 60 km BE 1 session
Cadence Maximum from a standing position	Gear ratio 6.2–7.2 m (e.g., 52 x 18 – 52 x 15 [racing bike])
Methods	Interval method (short intervals), rest length 3–5 min (with lactate accumulation 1–2 min)
Periodization	In PP II and III and in the CP, particularly important in the preparation of downhills and winding cross-country courses with several accelerations
Cyclization	Recommended during CP on Tuesdays or also Wednesdays
Organization forms	Training alone: monitor intensity by timing (6–8 sec) Group training: increases motivation, makes it easier to keep going during the reps
Course/Terrain	Both on- and off-road Also undulating courses
Mountain bike/ Racing bike	Both mountain bike and racing bike
Tips	Maximum pedaling but for only 6, at most 8 seconds, but at 100% effort; start off with easy pace; speed is not a monitoring parameter; perform regularly; very well-suited to off-road biking

Fig. 3.16: Speed strength training (PP: preparation phase; CP: competition phase)

A typical speed strength training workout is intervals of about 1:30–2 minutes in length (about 1 km) with low gear ratios and maximum cadence. Other speed strength training methods are so-called windsprints, or ins and outs. They involve riding 6–12 times about 20–30 meters, with an easy gear ratio, pedaling very gently for about 50 meters between sprints. Doing this workout on a gentle downhill slope or with a following wind enables you to train at very high cadences with low energy expenditure (small gear ratios).

Speed Strength or Sprint Training (SS)

Speed strength training serves primarily to improve sprinting and acceleration ability and corresponds to the anaerobic alactic metabolism. Starting from a very slow pace or a standstill and with average gear ratios, pedal as fast as possible for 6–8 seconds and then slow down again, and repeat after 1–2 minutes. The fatigue and lactic acid accumulate during the set and the CP and ATP reserves are completely emptied due to the short recovery times.

If the alactic acid energy supply is to be trained in isolation, the recovery periods must be extended to 3–5 minutes. This type of training should be part of every downhiller's training plan.

Training Programs

Sample training sessions for the different training zones can be found below, as evidence shows that many mountain bikers find it difficult to choose the right kind of workload for their performance level. Please bear in mind that the training suggestions are just that, suggestions, and are just intended to be a guide for trying out unfamiliar training methods. Your own creativity in modifying them should be limited only by training method boundaries.

The duration and training method are provided for each workout, and the rest times are also given for the interval and repetition methods. Further information like cadence, heart rate and gear ratio can be found in the tables relating to each training zone.

The training sessions are divided into three or four different performance levels. Usually, training zones should be trained in blocks, and the figures provided each correspond to an average training load within the block. So for block planning, all you need to do is to choose a load below and above the one provided, not exceeding loading increases of 15–30%.

The performance categories are listed below and are grouped according to physiology and the training loads performance structure in specific performance levels and age groups. This classification is for guidance purposes only and may be varied.

a. Hobby and fitness cycling
b. Youth (ages 15 and 16)
c. Juniors (ages 17 and 18)/women/marathon bikers
d. Men

CT (no block training)

CT a	30–40 min	continuous endurance method
CT b	40–60 min	continuous endurance method
CT c, d	60–90 min	continuous endurance method

BE 1

The shorter BE 1 workouts are also performed by mountain bikers in the men's category.

BE 1 a	1–2 hrs	continuous endurance method (fartlek)
BE 1 b	2–4 hrs	continuous endurance method (fartlek)
BE 1 c	4–6 hrs	continuous endurance method
BE 1 d	> 6 hrs	continuous endurance method

A training session in the following intensity zone is always preceded by a 20–30 minute BE 1 as a warm-up. The active recovery is BE 1/CT. After the more intense workouts, a 20–30 minute cool-down should be performed.

BE 2

BE 2 a	3-4 x 5–10 min	interval method (LI) with 5-min active rest
BE 2 b	3-4 x 10–15 min	interval method (LI) with 5-min active rest
BE 2 c	3-6 x 15–20 min	interval method (LI) with 5-min active rest
BE 2 d	3-6 x 20–30 min	interval method (LI) with 5-min active rest

RSE

Race-specific endurance can be trained using the interval, competition and repetition methods. The competition method is described here. All categories should train for both shorter and longer periods.

RSE a	10–20 min	competition method
RSE b	10–30 min	competition method
RSE c	10–40 min	competition method
RSE d	10–60 min	competition method

SE

The total time per workout can be split into up to four sessions if long mountains are available, in which case training follows the interval method.

SE a	15–20 min (3 x 5 min)	interval method	active rest 10 min
SE b	30–40 min (4 x 10 min)	interval method	active rest 10 min
SE c	40–60 min (4 x 15 min)	interval method	active rest 15 min
SE d	60–90 min (3 x 30 min)	interval method	active rest 20 min

ST

ST a	3–4 x 1:00–1:30 min	interval method (med)	active rest 5 min
ST b	3 – 4 x 1:30–2:00 min	interval method (med)	active rest 5 min
ST c	4 – 6 x 1:30–2:00 min	interval method (med)	active rest 5 min
ST d	6 – 8 x 2:30–3:30 min	interval method (med)	active rest 5 min

SS

SS a	6–8 x 6–8 sec	interval method (short)	active rest 1–5 min
SK b	8–10 x 6–8 sec	interval method (short)	active rest 1–5 min
SS c	10–12 x 6–8 sec (1 – 2 sets)	interval method (short)	active rest 1–5 min
SS d	10–12 x 6–8 sec (2–3 sets)	interval method (short)	active rest 1–5 min

3.3 Heart Rate Training

Intensity monitoring using the heart rate has the advantage of accuracy over subjective methods and allows fitness development and identifies any problems with form build-up. Unfortunately, the heart rate is also vulnerable to a range of variable disturbances, but with a little experience, they can be identified and analyzed.

The individual training zones can be calculated using simple formulas.

The History of Heart Rate Measurement for Training Monitoring

Twenty-five years ago, training monitoring using the heart rate was not accurate at all, as the heart rate could only be measured by taking the pulse at certain points of the body (wrist and neck), so continuous heart rate measurement was impossible. After that, heart rate monitors that appeared were only used by top athletes, who were also able to achieve great success using this method. The unbelievable success of the East German cyclists was based, among other things, on the consistent development and application of heart-rate-oriented training. Already in the mid-70s the first trials were being made there with wireless heart rate monitors. In the mid-80s, the first completely functional heart rate monitors by Polar hit the market, and today the heart rate monitor is an essential training monitoring tool available to all (around $60). Heart rate monitors are now used by everyone from World Cup pros to hobby cyclists.

In the early years, there was a lack of agreement concerning which heart rates to train with, but since then, many mountain bikers have mastered the use of the heart rate monitor and used it to structure their training a great deal more effectively.

How a Heart Rate Monitor Works

The heart rate is picked up by a transmitter secured in a chest strap and transmitted wirelessly by radio to the watch (the receiver). The chest electrodes located in the strap capture the heart beat, using the ECG method and is the most accurate form of measurement.

GPS devices document training, including all heart rate data. The analysis software makes training recording and evaluation extremely easy.

It's impossible to imagine daily training without a heart rate monitor.

User-friendly models allow programming the desired training intensity zone and give an acoustic or visual signal if you exceed or drop below it. The top-of-the-range models by Polar allow you to store heart rate data and other performance parameters (e.g., speed and cadence) during training or racing. At home, this data can then be transferred to a computer, where they can be put into graph form and analyzed.

These figures provide important information for effective training monitoring. It is better to put the watch on the handle bar near the stem for better control. When using a heart rate monitor, it is important to position the strap correctly and not too tightly so as not to hinder breathing. The electrodes can only capture the heart rate if they are slightly damp. Either wet them with a little water prior to training, or ride for a few minutes until contact is obtained thanks to your natural sweat production.

In the immediate vicinity of strong power sources (e.g., high voltage cables or railway lines), the monitor may briefly register very high figures or stop altogether. Occasionally, in training in a peleton or in a group, individual transmitters and receivers can experience interference and disturbance, but this is prevented in newer models by a coding of the transmission frequency.

Heart Rate Behavior in Mountain Biking

In mountain biking, the heart rate— depending on the course profile, the weather and the road surface—is already subject to relatively high fluctuations. In modern training and science-goal oriented training, intensity is controlled by heart rate and not by speed, which even on flat terrain is not an indicator of intensity. The desired intensity can be found by adjusting gear ratio and cadence.

How does the heart rate monitor help?

When Intensity Is Too High

One necessary consequence of heart-rate-oriented training is that now you need to ride more slowly (e.g., into a headwind or downhill) so as not to exceed the desired intensity zone (e.g., BE 1). It is also useful for identifying an excessively high heart rate due to infections.

When Intensity Is Too Low

Certain training zones and methods must be performed at high and very high intensities that are hard to estimate without a heart rate monitor. Also, in a race situation, the monitor shows whether the body has something in reserve or the tempo must be reduced to avoid producing too much lactic acid. A prerequisite for this is, of course, the thorough research of your own heart rate behavior in training and, if possible, the identification of your anaerobic threshold.

With a little experience, the heart rate also provides information about the rider's physical condition. To find this, it is necessary to have observed heart rate under different loads and at rest.

Naturally, the heart rate zones must not be seen as boundaries that are set in stone and must never be crossed. Deviations are occasionally allowed, if necessary. Just make sure that the majority of the workout takes place in the targeted zones as planned (usually BE 1).

Deviation—Resting Heart Rate

To first familiarize yourself with the heart rate monitor, you should measure your resting heart rate. The resting heart rate is not just an indicator of endurance fitness; it is a useful indicator of developing illness, infection or overtraining.

To be able to spot changes, you need to take your resting pulse rate in bed before getting up in the morning every day. If your resting heart rate normally varies, for example between 45 and 48 bpm, and then one morning you measure it at 55 bpm, this is a probably indication that you are coming down with an illness, even though no symptoms are noticeable yet. If the resting heart rate rises slowly during the day, this is usually an indication of overtraining; in any case, recovery is disrupted. After hard racing or on stage races, the resting heart rate is often slightly raised due to the extreme effort and very short recovery times. In general, an upward deviation of 6–8 bpm is a sign that the above factors should be checked and that you not push yourself too hard, particularly if the exercise heart rate is also higher than normal, and may even need to drop out of the race, because endurance training with an infection can damage the heart muscle and other organs.

As shown in figure 3.18, the resting heart rate usually increases during a training camp (by 1-2 bpm). However, the curve represents the group mean of a well-trained group. An unfit mountain biker would have a greater increase in resting heart rate after performing the same workout. Training workload must absolutely be adapted to performance level in order to avoid too high an increase and, therefore, a big recovery deficit in a basic training camp.

	Heart Rate	Cause	Remedy
Before	Increased resting HR	• Infection • Fatigue • Overstraining • Overtraining	• Break from training • Rehabilitation training • Visit to doctor
	Slight variation in resting HR	• Need for recovery • Infection	• Compensatory training • Rest
During	Unusually low maximum HR and general downward shift of HR; HR does not oscillate.	• Start of overtraining • Recovery deficit • Glycogen depletion	• Break from training • Compensatory training • BE 1 training
	Unusually high exercise HR	• Infection • Lack of fluid	• Possible repeat build-up training • Fluid intake
After	Unusually strong lowering of recovery HR	• Different manifestation of overtraining	• Reduce training or rest • Rehabilitation training
	Increased HR after training or racing over a long period of time (several hours)	• Extreme fatigue • Incipient infection • Lack of fluid	• Recovery measures • Fluid intake

Fig. 3.17: Heart rate fluctuations before, during and after training

Fig. 3.18: Change in resting heart rate during a 14-day basic training camp (averages of 12 participants)

Establishing Training Zones

Most of the training zones described in the previous chapter use the heart rate for monitoring purposes. The values shown correspond to an 18–35–year–old mountain biker in good physical shape with a maximum pulse rate of about 200. Younger and older mountain bikers, and also athletes with varying maximum heart rates, should not use these figures, because they would not be training in the correct zone.

That is why each training zone should be established by performance analysis or by using the maximum heart rate.

Determining Maximum Heart Rate (MHR)

The most accurate and safest way to determine training zones is to measure the MHR during a performance test under medical supervision. More senior mountain bikers (over the age of 40) and beginners should not carry out this test alone but only under medical supervision due to the risks involved.

Measuring the MHR would be too risky for rehabilitation cyclists, who should calculate their MHR according to the formula **220 − age = MHR**, or using accurate medical testing.

This formula provides only a very rough approximation (+/− 10) and should definitely not be used by elite bikers.

The test to establish maximum heart rate can be begun after a 30-minute warm-up.

With the Bike

To reach your maximum heart rate, increase the workload over a period of several minutes (about 4–5 min) and then pedal at maximum intensity for one more minute. A mountain with a gentle incline about 3–4 kilometers (2–2.5 mi) in length is ideal for this. It should be tackled at race pace using race gear ratios. The last 600 meters (660 yds) should be a flat-out, 100% effort final spurt in order to attain your maximum heart rate.

A high movement frequency (i.e., cadence) is necessary to achieve MHR. The heart rate is highest shortly after the end of the test.

In most cases, MHR is roughly 220 − age, but there are exceptions, as trained mountain bikers often have a MHR of about 200 up to the age of 35 or even older.

The only way to measure it accurately enough is with a heart rate monitor, and it is also required as the state of extreme exhaustion at the end of the test makes it impossible to measure the very high pulse manually.

As MHR values vary from sport to sport, depending on the amount of muscle mass recruited, MHR tests should also be conducted in your main cross-training sports, but definitely for cycling. Poor technique may prevent you from reaching your MHR in technically demanding sports such as inline skating or cross-country skiing.

Calculating the Intensity Zones

Establishing the training zones using this simple method is a real alternative to the expensive and difficult to interpret performance testing, although this is more accurate and mainly used at elite level. But even good mountain bikers can use the method presented here with no problem. The formulas used to calculate the intensity zones draw on many years of comprehensive studies of endurance athletes and are very accurate.

The exercise heart rate is calculated using the resting heart rate and the maximum heart rate and an intensity factor expressed as a percentage.
Step 1: Subtract the resting heart rate from the MHR.
Step 2: Multiply this figure by the intensity factor.
Step 3: The resting heart rate is added to the result.

Example:
1. 200 – 45 = 155
2. 155 x 0.52 = 80.6
3. 80.6 + 45 = 125.6

The calculated figure would be the upper heart rate limit for compensatory training (recovery training) for the person concerned.

Table 3.1: Intensity Factors

Compensatory zone	CT	Up to 0.52
Basic endurance 1	BE 1	0.52–0.65
Basic endurance 2	BE 2	0.65–0.82
Race-specific endurance	RSE	0.75–0.95
Strength endurance	SE	0.75–0.90
Speed training	ST	0.85–1.00
Speed strength training	SS	0.85–0.95

The factors represent the lower and upper limits of each zone. Correct intensity management is particularly important in the compensatory zone and the basic endurance zone.

In the last three specific high-intensity training zones (**SE**, **ST** and **SS**), training is managed less according to heart rate and more according to specific gear ratio data, cadences and movement tasks for pre-determined time or distance intervals, as a heart rate of 180, for example, can be attained by different training methods and workloads. However, even in these cases, the correct level of exertion is usually not reflected in the heart rate.

3.4   Performance Testing

Performance testing is a very complex subject that can only be touched upon in this book. This book does not go into detail regarding the different testing procedures.

It would probably be too difficult for the self-coached mountain biker to interpret the performance testing results, and he would need to consult an expert straight away. Many private training advisory institutes now conduct performance diagnostic testing. Universities also often require endurance-trained study participants. This is a good way to get this analysis done free of charge, but can be very time-consuming.

Mountain bikers with little time available for training, those who lack training motivation and beginners tend to expect miracles from performance testing. However, there is no escaping the fact that top performances cannot be achieved without a high training workload and a certain training age, particularly in cross-country.

3.4.1   Lab Testing

At elite level, four to six tests are carried out annually, at the start and in the middle of the preparation phase and at the start and middle of the racing phase. Performance testing is used in preparing for peak performances in order to be able to identify and correct any weak points in good time.

A single test does not reveal enough information for training, so regular testing is required to be able to benefit fully from performance testing. The purpose of lab performance tests is to monitor training planning to enable optimal training structuring. Control parameters are the heart rate and lactate concentration, not cycling speed.

Stage Test

The athlete exercises to the point where he is forced to drop out due to exhaustion and gradually increases the intensity in stages on an individually adjusted bike ergometer. Depending on the test protocol and purpose, the stages last between two and four minutes with load increases of 20–50 watts per level. A recent tendency has been to reduce the load increases per minute. A standard test protocol starts at 100 watts and increases by 20 watts every three minutes.

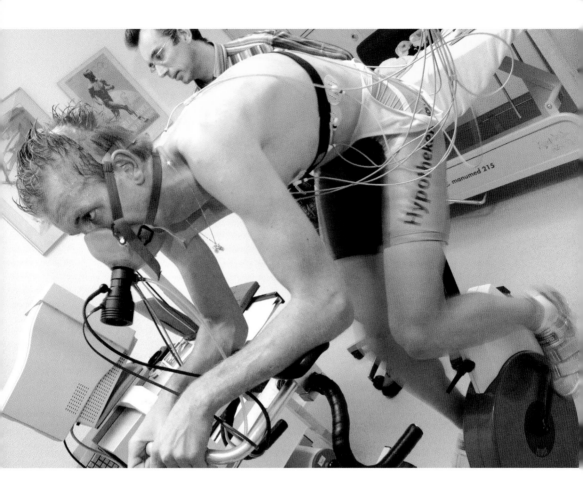

This allows lactate and heart rate behavior to be tracked very accurately. Tests with increases of 40 watts and more every three minutes are no longer considered suitable but are still used in the commercial field as they take less time to perform.

In order to ensure the comparability of the tests, they must be conducted under standardized conditions, since the test results are strongly influenced by the previous day's diet and training and the method used for measuring lactate values.

Measurements to establish physiological and biomechanical data such as heart rate, electrocardiogram (ECG), cadence, power, oxygen intake, minute volume and lactic acid, urea and creatine kinase concentrations can be carried out during the test.

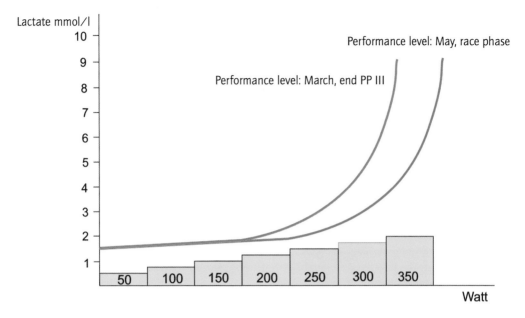

Fig. 3.19: Lactate performance curve established during laboratory-based stage test

A more detailed explanation of the stage test procedure would exceed the scope of this book, as such tests cannot be self-administered anyway.

The most important measurements, which ultimately are also interconnected, are power, heart rate and the associated lactate values, as well as spiroergometric parameters, if needed. If these are represented graphically, we obtain the so-called **lactate performance curve** (see figure 3.19), which is used to calculate the aerobic and anaerobic thresholds.

Aerobic and Anaerobic Thresholds
The aerobic threshold for the endurance-trained mountain biker is on average between approximately 1.5 and 2.5 millimoles lactate per liter of blood, and the anaerobic is between 3.5 and 4.5 millimoles/liter; although the views of sports science, however, diverge quite considerably on this point. It is more accurate to calculate the individual thresholds. As shown infigure 3.20, exercise below the aerobic threshold is performed purely aerobically, between the thresholds the mixed metabolism prevails and above the anaerobic threshold the anaerobic metabolism predominates. A longer load above the anaerobic threshold necessarily entails a lactate build-up, which means that after a short time (a few seconds to several minutes) the athlete is forced to stop.

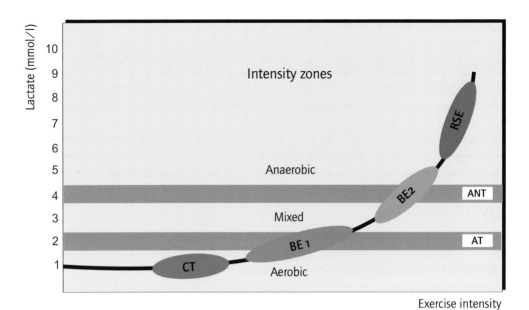

Fig. 3.20: Threshold model and intensity zones. The thresholds are shown as thick shadowed lines whose width corresponds to the possible range of the figures. The intensity zones are represented schematically. AT: aerobic threshold; ANT: anaerobic threshold.

Interpretation

The interpretation involves relating the heart rate and power to the lactate values and then calculating the individual thresholds. Performance development in general and performance improvement in particular can be accurately traced by viewing several lactate curves.

Once the factors that influence test results have been disregarded, lab testing, when correctly conducted, is the most accurate method of determining the training zones and is the only way of identifying and quantifying the peak performance capacity.

Other Lab Tests

The complex, cycling-specific performance diagnostic analysis not only enables the measurement of the overall performance on the bike but also makes it possible to investigate separate elements of the overall performance using specific tests. The following list conveys the variety of possible test: maximum pedaling power, maximum cadence, anaerobic capacity, pulling power as a function of cadence and pedaling power for different types of effort.

3.4.2 Field Test

The field test is a stage test (i.e., gradual increase in effort) that is not conducted in a lab under standardized and idealized conditions but performed in the field (i.e., with your own bike on the roads, in the forest or on the track).

Due to differing external factors (e.g., wind, course, temperature, equipment and tire pressure), it is very hard to compare several tests by the same athlete or simultaneous test by different athletes. If possible, the field test can be conducted on a cycle race track. It's always the same lap length, wind can be calculated and is easy to perform).

In the field test, normally only two or three parameters are determined (e.g., the heart rate and the lactate value as a function of speed).

The intensity during the test is either controlled by speed or heart rate, with stage lengths of 4–6 kilometers. The long stages are better for very well-trained cyclists to determine training intensities. For example, start with a speed of 30 kilometers/hour that is increased every 2.5 kilometers (for a 250 m track = 10 laps) by 2 kilometers/hour. During the test, the heart rate is shown on the heart rate monitor, and after each stage the lactate values are also measured. It is the cyclist's responsibility to stick as closely as possible to the speed or heart rate targets with the aid of their bike computers or heart rate monitors.

Heart Rate Method
If the loading target is the heart rate, a little feeling for pace and physical awareness and, above all, experience of heart-rate-oriented intensity control are required. The first stage should be clearly in the aerobic zone and so should the second. The third stage should be in the mixed zone and the fourth stage just below the anaerobic threshold. The last stage can cross into the anaerobic zone. The heart rate sequence of 115–130–145–160–175–190 is a tried and tested one. Due to the exponential increase in air resistance when cycling at high speeds, the heart rate method is preferable to the speed method.

Cadence
In field tests it can be difficult to choose the correct gear ratio to enable the cadence in all stages to remain at a constant 80–100 revolutions/minute, hence the need for a cadence meter. This means small gear ratios for lower speeds and big gear ratios for high speeds, and it is difficult to adapt them to the exact velocity or heart rate required.

The Cross-Trainer by *Polar* is very suitable for use in a field test, because it also records the speed and cadence as well as the heart rate.

A field test can also be performed on the mountain bike on a flat circuit on good, country lanes that are sheltered from the wind.

Analysis

To start with, plot a graph with the lactate concentration on the vertical axis and the heart rate on the horizontal axis. On the x-coordinate enter the speed (calculate for every stage). Now the individual data pairs are populated. It creates two data rows: the lactate-speed data row and the heart rate-speed data row. Two curves are formed by connecting the points on a data row.

The curve is interpreted by relating a specific lactate value to the corresponding heart rate on the other curve. For example, the aerobic threshold might lie at a heart rate of 130 bpm. This means that in basic training 1, the heart rate of 130 bpm should not be exceeded.

The aerobic threshold corresponds to the lowest measurement in the lactate-speed curve, provided that it was measured accurately. The anaerobic threshold is calculated by adding 1.5 millimoles/liter lactate to the aerobic threshold figure.

The other training zones are calculated using the lactate values provided in the respective illustrations.

3.4.3   A Simple Test to Determine the Anaerobic Threshold

Cross-country races use the aerobic–anaerobic mixed metabolism. This means that the heart rate, depending on course profile and race duration, fluctuates around the anaerobic threshold but is usually slightly below. You can take advantage of this in order to determine the anaerobic threshold, at least approximately, in a time-trial test.

You will need a heart rate monitor with a memory (e.g., Cross-Trainer or Vantage by Polar) and a suitable computer interface in order to be able to download the memory contents to a computer and analyze them.

Perform a time-trial either on the mountain bike on flat paths or roads or on a racing bike on flat roads. Choose a course on which you don't need to slow the pace due to traffic lights or other obstacles. A circuit of 5 kilometers is ideal.

Different Course Lengths

The anaerobic threshold should be tested over distances of 5, 10 and 40 kilometers (3, 6.2 and 25 mi). These tests should not take longer than 9, 18 and 75 minutes, respectively. The test can be performed as a race or as a training session. Motivation is better if done as a race, which is why faster times and also higher heart rate can be aimed for.

How to Do It

After doing the time-trial, calculate the average heart rate for the whole of the time-trial using the heart rate analysis program on the computer. This value is divided by the appropriate percentage found in the following diagram. The result is a value for the anaerobic threshold that is approximate, though very often fairly accurate. It is most accurate for the long 40-kilometer distance, in which the exercise heart rate corresponds to the anaerobic threshold if the cyclist is motivated.

Example:

A biker covers a 10-km time-trial in 15 minutes, with an average heart rate of 182 bpm.

Calculation: 182 divided by 1.07 equals 170 bpm as the threshold figure. A 40-kilometer time-trial or a cross-country race lasting roughly an hour should then be ridden at 100% of the threshold heart rate (i.e., 170 bpm).

What's the point of all this?

Because cross-country races are often very similar to time-trials, knowing your anaerobic threshold is very helpful when it comes to choosing the correct intensity during the race. In races up to a length of about one and a half hours, you should try to ride a threshold heart rate pace. In longer races, the target heart rate should be a few beats per minute slower and, in longer races, a few beats per minute faster.

Distance	Race	Training
5 km/3 miles	110% of ANT	104% of ANT
10 km/6.2 miles	107% of ANT	102% of ANT
40 km/25 miles	100% of ANT	97% of ANT

Fig. 3.21: The anaerobic threshold heart rate derived from the average exercise heart rate in time-trials.

On inclines, before descents and in attacks, it is possible for the heart rate to be higher than the threshold pulse rate, as the descent gives you the chance to recover a little. The anaerobic threshold can also be used to determine training zones so that below 73% of the anaerobic threshold is compensatory training, between 72 and 84% is basic endurance zone 1, from 84–97% is basic endurance 2 and up to 104% is race-specific endurance.

Off-Road Time-Trials: A Simple Performance Test

The racing method is the simplest kind of performance test, and it should be performed regularly. Only by knowing how it feels to ride at your endurance limit (and the heart rate required to do so) and frequently experiencing race-specific situations can you completely fulfill your performance potential in races. Challenging, race-length, off-road time-trials teach you how to better gauge your performance ability and thereby identify your optimal race heart rate. Heart rate monitors with a memory facility and appropriate computer software are very useful for this as they allow you to analyze races retrospectively. So after about 20 races and time-trials, it is possible to determine your optimal rate heart rate for different race durations and types.

3.5   Periodization: The Training Year

In endurance sports, the year is divided into different training phases with different contents and targets. A training year, unlike the calendar year, usually starts with the first preparation phase in the fall. The division of the different phases is determined by the racing season, which in the case of mountain biking lasts from April to October. Although racing may take place during the other months, races are thin on the ground and not important. In the sports of cross-country skiing or cycling, the preparation phase is in spring with the race phase in winter. However, the following advice assumes that the racing phase is in the summer.

The target of periodization is to attain peak race fitness (taking into account time available for training and other circumstances). At international elite level, periodization is often tailored to one single race, for example the World Championships or the Olympic Games. Even at national level, though, riders prepare specifically for certain championships or important races.

A true champion of this planned form build-up is Dutch mountain bike racer Bart Brentjens, who has managed to hit peak form at exactly at these times on several occasions.

	PP I	PP II	PP III	RP	TP
Duration	6-9 weeks	6-9 weeks	4-6 weeks	19-23 weeks	3-6 weeks
Training zones	BE 1 (BE 2)	BE 1 BE 2 (RSE) SE ST	CT BE 1 BE 2 RSE SE ST SS	CT BE 1 BE 2 RSE SE ST SS	CT BE 1
Training types	• MTB • (Racing bike) • Cross-training • Indoor training • Fitness studio/weights room • Technique training • Team games • Squash, Badminton Stretching Recovery circuit	• MTB • Racing bike • Cross-training • Indoor training • Fitness studio/weights room • Technique training • Team games • Squash, Badminton Stretching Recovery circuit	• MTB • Racing bike • Cross-training • (Indoor training) • Fitness studio/weights room • Technique training • Team games • Squash, Badminton Stretching Recovery circuit	• MTB • Racing bike • Cross-training (a compensating sport) • (Indoor training) • Fitness studio/weights room • Technique training Stretching Recovery circuit	• Fun activities • Cross-training • Team games Stretching
Methods	• Endurance methods	• Endurance methods • Interval method • Repetition method • (Race method)	• Endurance methods • Interval method • Repetition method • Race method	• Endurance methods • Interval method • Repetition method • Race method	• Endurance methods
Targets	◄ • General performance foundations	◄ • General performance foundations ◄ • Special performance foundations	◄ • General performance foundations ◄ • Special performance foundations • Shaping of racing fitness	◄ • Shaping and stabilizing of racing fitness ◄ • Special performance foundations	• Recovery • Mental break
Errors	• Too much volume • Intensity too high • Boring training	• Intensity too high • Recovery too short • Lack of strength training • Boring training	• Lack of strength training • Recovery too short • No periodization • Boring training	• Too little volume • Recovery too short • Poor choice of race • Boring training	• Complete break from training • Continued bike training • Intensity too high

Fig. 3.2.2: Periodization overview

To do this, Brentjens subordinated all training and particularly all racing to the attainment of his seasonal goal, which explains his more than modest results in the early World Cup races. Only a few weeks before the main race of the season did he come into form in time to hit peak form at the World Championships and Olympic Games.

In the sport of road-cycle racing, Miguel Indurain Larraya was an expert of tapering (race preparation), and his annual periodization was specifically oriented to the goal of winning the Tour de France. This single peak method of periodization can increasingly be seen in international endurance sport, as the race calendar is becoming longer and longer and the cyclist must focus on quite specific, commercially significant main races. With the standard of international mountain bike race fields constantly improving, it has now become almost impossible to be in winning form during the whole season.

This preparation for a race or a short peak performance phase of two to four weeks can also be copied by the average mountain biker or marathon biker.

The classic order of phases is: preparation phases I-III, race phase, transition phase. If you are using a double peak periodization, the duration of each phase is reduced and usually each phase performed twice but with specifically adapted content for each race phase.

Road pro Gerald Ciolek training in the sports hall

A sequence for double-peak periodization goes as follows:

Preparation phases I and II, race phase I, transition phase I, preparation phases III and IV, rrace phase II, transition phase II.

This type of double-peak periodization is often undertaken by cyclists contesting road cycling seasons followed by a track or cross-country season; by mountain bikers (although rarely) contesting summer and winter seasons; or in other sports, such as track and field athletics, soccer or ski jumping all of which have summer and winter seasons. Many top mountain bikers start off in cross-country biking and after the MTB season complete another cross-country season until the end of January to mid-February.

Attaining world-class performances with double-peak periodization is generally very difficult in mountain biking in particular and endurance sport in general, as the shortened recovery phases negatively impact individual peak performance development.

The contents and training goals of the different phases are described briefly next.

3.5.1 Preparation Phase (PP)

The purpose of the preparation phases is to create basic but also special performance prerequisites with a view to attaining race fitness.

At the start of the training year—roughly in November after a regenerative transition phase—the training focus is on regaining or maintaining basic endurance ability. Use as many different training methods as possible throughout winter training. The intensities are low, and intensive training sessions should be well-spaced but not be omitted completely.

At the start of the preparation phase and, in particular, preparation phase I, training should be structured, but it is not necessary to stick to a rigid plan. A flexible weekly plan with a basic workload that can be augmented according to desire and time available is recommended.

Cross-Training
A fantastic way of improving basic endurance in mountain biking is cross-training (i.e., carrying out many different endurance sports that all have the goal of improving basic endurance and also, to some extent, strength endurance). The advantages of cross-training are: firstly, from a mental point of view, it brings variety and prevents training being boring and, secondly, the muscles and metabolism are exercised differently. Some great cross-training sports are:

Inline skating, cross-country skiing, roller skating, aqua-jogging, swimming, aerobics, running, hiking, mountain climbing and other endurance sports.

The advantages of cross-training:
- Improvement of movement learning and physical awareness
- Development of new performance reserves
- Mental balance
- Active recovery
- Prevention of one-sided loading

Running

Running or jogging is particularly suitable for winter training, as well as being a year-round training method for mountain bikers with racing ambitions. A great advantage of running is that it can be done in bad weather, after dark, and even on the shortest days of winter; once you are familiar with the route, you can run on level paths in the dark with no problem. This allows you to continue winter training, which is essential in the preparation phase.

If you run very little or not at all during the racing season, do not rush into running. To start with, keep the runs short (no longer than 30 mins) and the intensity low and gradually increase the frequency. By respecting these rules, you can usually avoid lower-limb orthopedic problems.

A prerequisite for healthy and effective running training is suitable shoes that support the feet according to their shape (e.g., supination and pronation). Get advice in a specialist shoe shop and preferably pay a bit more for good running shoes, which should also be replaced regularly.

You should run in a loose, flowing style with strides that are not too long, an upright upper body and slightly bent arms. The short strides reduce the shock load compared to long strides. Runs on forest or country paths are ideal. Trail running also has a good training effect and, more importantly, is fun. Runs between 45 and 90 min (for men) are optimal. Younger cyclists can run for up to an hour. The training heart rate during basic endurance training runs is slightly higher than on the bike. Finally, the running action intensively stretches the leg muscles.

A variant of running is **Nordic walking**, or pole running. This involves running uphill (field or path) while simulating cross-country skiing by propelling forward forcefully with ski poles. Nordic walking is very intensive and also trains the trunk and arm muscles.

Orienteering is another variant. This is an independent sport in which you run through the countryside from one set point to another using a map and compass, and you get a stamp at each checkpoint. Like mountain biking, orienteering is a great way to experience nature, but nature must be respected and not damaged in the process.

Mountain hikes can last for several hours, as can **climbing tours**. Both are excellently suited to improving basic endurance. The low intensity particularly activates the fat-burning metabolism.

Aqua-Jogging

Aqua-jogging is another form of running, in which the athlete floats in the water with the aid of a buoyancy vest, and only his head and shoulders stick out of the water. Using a technique that is easy to learn under instruction, you move forward slowly in the water. Different loading forms are possible. From rehab training to basic training to high-intensity training with anaerobic mobilization, all are possible.

In many endurance sports and particularly in running, aqua-jogging is used as a low impact training alternative. Also in other sports, aqua-jogging is used early on in rehab training, when normal running training is still impossible due to injury.

Technique

With the upper body leaning slightly forward, simulate a running action by kicking away the water with your feet. Swing the arms back and forth next to the body like a normal running action, using different possible hand positions to provide differing resistance. An aqua-jogging workout lasts about one hour; after a 10-minute warm-up, you can either perform different intervals or train according to the endurance method. A few coordination exercises and functional strengthening of the core and arm muscles round off the session before a cool-down (10 min).

Swimming

Traditional swimming training is also a good form of compensatory training for the mountain biker. The lack of impact makes it particularly suitable for the post-injury rehabilitation phase. However, correct technique is important. Breast stroke should be avoided due to the same physiologically unsound spine position (overextension of the cervical spine) as in cycling and the sometimes harmful shearing motion of the legs. Front or back crawl are preferable, both of which serve to build up muscular weaknesses of little-used muscles in the arms and trunk.

Swimming training is usually done according to the endurance method, in which distances of between 1,000 and 3,000 meters (660–3300 yds) are covered. It is important to familiarize yourself slowly with the demands of the sport.

In swimming and aqua-jogging, it should be noted that due to the hydrostatic pressure of water, the heart rate at the same metabolic load (same intensity level) is about 10 bpm lower than on dry land.

Fin Swimming

A variation of swimming that is quite rare and particularly interesting for mountain bikers and other cyclists is fin swimming, which mainly works the leg and gluteus muscles. The lower movement frequency and the greater motion resistance involved in fin swimming provide a very useful strength endurance workout. The training method of choice is the endurance method, lasting between 30 and 90 minutes.

Inline Skating

Inline skating is growing in popularity and not just as a hobby but also as an elite sport. Speed skating is the racing version, in which proper races are carried out on fenced off circular courses. What makes inline skating so well-suited for mountain bikers' basic endurance and strength endurance training is that the leg muscles work in a similar way to the pedaling action in cycling. The main contraction type of the muscles in skating is concentric, as in cycling, and the leg extension is performed at similar angles. There is also a significant strength endurance component due to the long support phase and the low movement frequency. The static postural muscles, particularly those in the back, are also worked hard.

The movement structure of inline skating is almost identical to that of ice speed skating. Many ice speed skaters train in summer with the mountain bike, racing bike and inline skates. In the Netherlands and the USA, inline races are even organized specifically for cyclists and cycling races for ice speed skaters and inline skaters. Ingrid Haringa is one of many famous cyclists who have reached elite level both on the ice and on the bike.

If you would like to take inline skating seriously as a training form, it is better to purchase skates with a long blade with five wheels for speed skating, but they are not cheap.

A training session with skates lasts roughly 45 minutes to 2 hours and should be done on roads that are as traffic-free and flat as possible. Another good workout is frequently covering a circuit a few miles long, particularly for group training sessions.

The heart rate for basic training lies in roughly the same zone as for cycling training. Intervals and sprints can also be performed on skates.

Cross-Country Skiing

Cross-country skiing, like Nordic walking, solicits a very high proportion of the body's muscles. As well as arms, shoulders and legs, the back and stomach muscles are also worked hard. In cross-country skiing, a correct technique is necessary for successful and effective training.

In cross-country skiing, there are two different techniques: the classic, or diagonal technique, which is very similar to Nordic walking and the newer skating technique, in which the leg action is very similar to that in inline skating and ice speed skating, with an arm action is based on the double-pole push of the classic technique. While classic ski tracks can be found in almost all winter sports resorts, skating tracks are few and far between. This is why most bikers come to cross-country skiing with the classic running style and later, if they are so inclined, they can learn the considerably faster skating technique, which also requires special equipment.

For those who do not live in the mountains or near winter sports resorts, cross-country skiing is the best sport for a winter vacation. Two weeks in January or February with two to four hours of cross-country skiing daily lay a good foundation for the increasing workload that is to follow when you return home.

For workouts lasting one to six hours, depending on intensity, the heart rates for the appropriate intensity levels roughly correspond to those for running and are higher than for biking. In cross-country skiing, the temptation is to run with very high intensity, partly because of the sheer amount of muscle mass used (almost the whole body). This can be resolved by running longer distances, which are automatically tackled at a lower intensity.

Roller skiing is a proven basic training method. On special roller skis, one- to three-hour sessions can be carried out on flat terrain on traffic-free roads and lanes. Both the classic and the skating technique can be performed on modern roller skis. If you have already invested in inline skates, you can avoid splashing out on a pair of roller skis and just buy a pair of suitable, sufficiently long skating poles with special points for asphalt. With skates and poles you can easily simulate the skating technique. If you dare to venture into traffic with roller skis or skates, you must be able to skate, brake and dodge confidently, otherwise this could be very dangerous.

Nordic skating with FLEET skates is an ideal form of winter training for bikers.

Example Weekly Plans

The suggested weekly training plans designed for each training phase are intended for these cross-country biking categories: juniors, men, women, seniors and marathon bikers. For youth and keep-fit bikers, the number of workouts must be reduced. Volumes are not provided, just content and intensity. More precise training suggestions with concrete details can be found by consulting the training for each category.

Preparation Phase I (PP I)

PP I lasts from November until the end of December. Every two or three weeks of increasing volume is followed by a recovery week with a significantly lower workload. Within a week (microcycle), training follows the same principle: two or three days of increasing workload then one day of recovery training or rest. For those who are reluctant to follow such a program, PP I offers them the possibility of training in a less structured way; the only important thing is to train regularly and, at least in the men's category, about 5–6 times a week with a weekly volume of 8–12 hours. Finally, don't forget that training should also be fun and not just a chore.

The example weekly plan gives an overview of the training structure in this phase. The training blocks can of course exceed one week in length, depending on individual targets.

Fig. 3.23: Weekly cycle in PP I, two cross-training sessions (BE 1), one gym workout

In **PP I**, the basic fundamentals for sporting performance are formed, as previously described, and the focus of this phase is improving basic endurance, although strength, flexibility and coordination should not be neglected. These latter qualities can be developed through well-planned athletics training in the gym and weight room.

Winter indoor training comprises various games and special strength and endurance programs. After a long MTB season, the postural muscles need well-planned balancing and build-up training to avoid or compensate for postural defects. It is also a good time for the athlete to learn new strengthening and stretching exercises and to correct the execution of familiar ones.

Endurance training need not be done on the bike as long as you practice the other aforementioned endurance sports. Fun and playful mountain bike technique training is a good group activity.

The duration of the winter training sessions is considerably shorter than the summer ones, lasting between one and three, at most four, hours (road training or cross-country skiing), but the intensity is low. Training volume increases sharply toward the end of **PP I**.

Particularly for youngsters, the winter holidays are an excellent opportunity for a first training camp at home or away. The training is not as hard as at spring training camps, but the holidays at least allow for regular training with slightly higher volumes than before.

Preparation Phase II (PP II)

PP II starts in January and lasts until the end of February, depending on when your season starts. At first, there is no reduction in the other general training methods, but in this phase the specific training (i.e., bike training: MTB, road) does increase in the **BE 1** zone. Bike training does not start to gradually replace the other sports (e.g., cross-training) until February, although one or two cross-training sports should still be practiced during the season as compensatory sports. Strength training (February: maximum strength phase) and general athletic training (gym training) should be also continued. For periodization of strength training, see chapter 4.

As in **PP I**, two or three weeks of hard training are followed by one week of reduced training. If the holiday period was used as a training camp, the following week should be a recovery week. The weeks should now be subdivided into two and three-part blocks. The weekends, in particular, are perfect for a three-part block with longer **BE 1** sessions on the bike.

During **PP II**, training volume and frequency increase, but at first, the intensity remains mainly in the basic endurance zone. On weekdays, training should be done progressively in the **BE 2** zone; while at weekends, provided that a long three-part block is carried out, training remains in the BE 1 zone. This phase concludes with another rest week or a few days of reduced training for recovery.

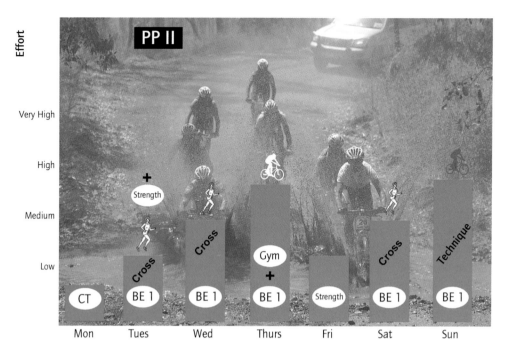

Fig. 3.24: Weekly cycle in PP II: two to three workouts as cross-training, the rest on the bike

Preparation Phase III (PP III)

PP III, which, depending on when the racing phase starts, lasts from the end of February to the end of March into mid-April (i.e., a period of 4–6 wks) and is used for the specific preparation of the racing phase.

Early preparation races can already be contested in **PP III**. It is absolutely possible to prolong **PP III** until the end of April, if **PP I** was started late or there is a late start to the season.

Usually, the spring training camp falls in **PP III**, which has a special chapter devoted to it (chapter 3.8). If a training camp is held in **PP III**, the preparation and recovery must be planned. Usually, two-week training camps are prepared for with a high-volume microcycle followed by a few rest days, followed by a compensation microcycle. These training camps are usually used to improve the aerobic capacity which is achieved by means of high training volumes.

During the rest of the **PP III** training weeks, training is high-volume and sometimes high-intensity. Try to schedule the high-intensity workouts after the recovery week following the training camp to form a seamless transition into the racing phase. RSE intervals and **ST–SS** training are ideal for this period, and strength endurance workouts on the bike should also be done more often now.

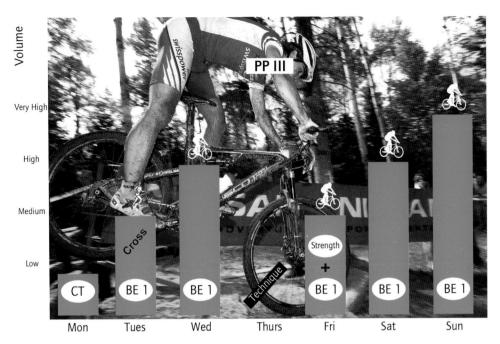

Fig. 3.25: Weekly cycle in PP III: focus on volume, one cross-training session (Tuesday or Friday) and the rest on the bike

This phase is also characterized by stopping gym training and one of the cross-training sessions. The training methods are now specific. Usually, the **PP III** is the phase with the highest training workload. The body can only cope with these high training loads if an appropriate foundation has been laid in the first two preparation phases. If this is not the case, the body will be overtaxed by the **PP III** training, leading to a significant recovery deficit, which will largely or even completely hinder the development of peak form.

Volumes are highest in BE training (e.g., up to seven hours per session for men). Training is again organized in two, three or even four-day blocks at elite level.

As mentioned, the first test races are performed in **PP III** in order to test fitness and to identify any weaknesses that can be addressed in subsequent microcycles.

Special bike training methods, such as **SE**, **ST**, **RSE** and **SS**, are best trained in two or three-day blocks. Strength endurance, for example, is trained on three consecutive days with more volume each day (e.g., 20, 30 then 40 min). Avoid combining the specific bike training methods, especially in the same workout.

3.5.2   Racing Phase (RP)

The racing phase is usually the longest phase, as it lasts from the end of April to the end of September or even longer. During these 19–23 weeks, cyclization must also be planned, as an ongoing form progression throughout this phase is impossible. Only a few other sports have such long racing phases as mountain biking and cycling, although many races are required in both sports to reach peak form.

The first weeks of the **RP** when the early races are contested are useful in volume-oriented training as an early test of form. Weaknesses and strengths can be spotted and analyzed.

In the coming weeks, you should try to use the cyclization format to correct particularly serious weaknesses, such as inadequate basic endurance, too little strength or poor anaerobic mobilization.

Forming Cycles
Subdivide the racing phase in exactly the same way as the other phases. Two to four (possibly five) progressively harder training weeks are followed by a recovery week with greatly reduced training. This cycle constitutes a block. Every block should be focused primarily on one target.

A good way of structuring this phase is to alternate phases focusing on volume and intensity. After three high-volume weeks, plan a few rest days and then two more weeks of more intensive training, followed by another recovery week. The recovery weeks in the **RP** are vital and must never be neglected.

Workload Increase to Seasonal Peak
The next block should have a higher overall workload. The overall workload is increased until the seasonal peak, right up to one week before the seasonal peak, when all training is in the **CT/BE 1** zone, apart from two moderately hard sessions on Wednesday and Thursday (Sunday: race).

The volume-focused weeks in the racing phase, unlike the volume-focused week in the preparation phases, are also replaced by intensive loads in the form of races. In addition, on the lower-volume training days (e.g., the first day in a three-day block), training should be more intensive.

Race-Free Phase

An effective training method, particularly if you have planned not only for two seasonal peaks, but also for single peaks, is the inclusion of a two- to four-week race-free phase that divides the racing phase in half. During this time, training is initially reduced, and then basic endurance training is progressively harder and improved. Fortunately, this race-free phase starts with the last week of a block (i.e., the recovery week). The structure follows the rehabilitation training in chapter 6.

Lots of Strength Endurance Training

Strength endurance training in the lower-intensity zone should be included in the volume blocks throughout this phase, because it is not very difficult at this lower intensity.

Regular gym or weight sessions should also be part of the performance-oriented biker's training program. See chapter 4 for more on this.

Technique Training

A technical component should always be included in mountain bike sessions, focusing on a specific technique. These exercises are not usually strenuous but should be carried out at the start of the workout in a rested state.

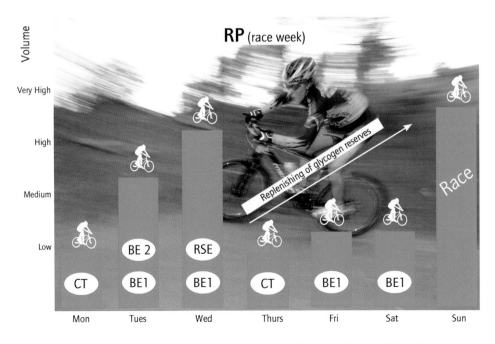

Fig. 3.26: Weekly cycle in the RP: pre-race week with hard training on Wednesday followed by a recovery phase

In addition, sessions focusing only on technique should be scheduled as the second session of the day. See chapter 8 for more on technique training.

Weekly Plan

In order to be able to perform successfully even in the preparatory or form-building races, each training week, or microcycle, must be structured. Weekly plan suggestions for each category can be found next.

The training workload must be reduced at the right time prior to a race in order to start the race fresh. If you compete in a race or a marathon on Sunday, the last strenuous workout should take place on Thursday (Wednesday), if the race is on Saturday, then on Wednesday (Tuesday). Some bikers also need longer recovery times, others shorter. You must experiment to see what works best for you. In the following days, Friday and Saturday, training is done in the **CT/BE 1** zones. The day before the race, you should definitely go riding. A short, intensive workout as a pre-race interval primes the body for the race, activates the metabolism and acts as a fitness check. It is also the chance for a last-minute equipment check.

Training Block with Races

Add a race to a training block to work harder and add variety. Start on a Friday with a medium-length workout, do a long ride at low intensity on Saturday, and on Sunday after the race, do another one to tow hours, ideally on the bike, on the way home. Make sure your carbohydrate intake is sufficient, especially on the Saturday.

A non-racing weekend should be used for an extra-long **BE 1** block.

Mondays Are Recovery Days

On Mondays, the focus should be on recovery. However, for form build-up, it is also possible to follow the race day with a very long **BE 1** session for a higher training workload.

3.5.3 Transition Phase (TP)

The transition phase is the time for recovery from the daily training and racing routine. At elite mountain biking level, this is usually vacation time. While training in the other phases is predominantly targeted and structured, in this phase, planning is avoided. You can do what you like. Low intensities and reduced volumes promote recovery. Although some athletes swear by a complete break from all sports for four weeks, for medical reasons you should remain active. Just avoid cycling during this time in order to raise your motivation for the coming preparation phases. The transition phase usually lasts about three to five weeks.

Many bikers even avoid bike training until the start of December or even later, just concentrating on cross-training in sports that they otherwise wouldn't have time for.

3.5.4   Running Training Throughout the Year

Year-Round Running Training
One training session per week of about one to two hours should also be reserved for cross-training. At least every two weeks, this session should consist of running, in order to prepare the muscles for the running element of races. If you neglect running now and also during the racing phase, you will pay the price in terms of serious muscle soreness or other leg injuries during the longer running sections of cross-country races. Regular running training also helps to develop a more economical running action. Running sessions can be included during the entire preparation phase and also in the summer as bad-weather training. The intensity should be adapted to the rest of the training, but not be too high.

3.5.5   MTB or Road Bike?

Bike Training With the MTB or Road Bike?
A hot topic is whether a mountain biker should train with a racing bike or whether peak performance can only be attained by training on the mountain bike. A look at the background will give us the answer.

   After the first mountain bike races were held and the sport of mountain biking began to be commercialized, the first road cyclists soon discovered mountain biking for themselves. Many, especially the less successful or those at the end of their careers, switched to mountain biking and mainly contested mountain biking races, where their superior fitness thanks to years of racing meant that the other mountain bikers didn't stand a chance.

Today, many coaches and scientists are of the opinion that in order to be successful in mountain biking, it is essential to train and even race on the road. Hardcore mountain bikers, though, prefer to do all their training on the mountain bike, where they believe similar training results as in combined training can be obtained. However, the fact is that almost all successful mountain bikers in the World Cup have come from road cycling or the sport of cross-country, but only in the rarest cases (actually in the sport of cross-country) do they reach the very top.

MTB World Cup in Spa-Francorchamps in Belgium

The road cyclists' success is definitely not because it is not possible to train as hard with the mountain bike. Their success is due to their participation in road races and circuit races. Their participation in road races, usually year-round, gives the road cyclists an advantage over mountain bikers in most areas of conditioning, except possibly coordination, and particularly in endurance and strength.

So it would seem that it is not basic training on the racing bike that gives the decisive advantage, but rather the participation in road races. The problem of doing basic endurance training off-road with the mountain bike can be solved by training with the mountain bike and smooth tires on the road, which has the same effect. However, mountain bikers with slicks are still not allowed to participate in the longer and more frequently held road races. Mountain bike races are usually too short and too intensive to be able to trigger the same metabolic and muscular adaptations as road races. So many factors would appear to indicate that it is impossible to reach the very top of mountain biking without training and racing on the road, unless youalready have several years of experience as a road cyclist behind you.

Mountain bikers ride on the roads, too: Lado Fumic with the race doctor during the Regio Tour.

Another problem encountered by bikers who only enter mountain bike races is the currently very sparse racing program compared to the road and the almost complete lack of stage races in which peak form can be developed.

Despite these compelling reasons, young cyclists should be allowed to choose freely between the MTB and the racing bike. Only from the junior age group onward should the coach stress the importance of the road bike if the biker is talented and ambitious.

As already described, in the discipline of cross-country, as on the track, there is a performance explosion to be reckoned with as soon as good road pros start contesting mountain bike races. Road pros with many thousands of miles of racing in classics and stage races under their belts would be superior to the current MTB pros over technically undemanding courses.

It is therefore advisable for elite mountain bikers to join a road team and enter important preparation races on the road and if possible also stage races, in order to have as much mileage as possible in their legs before key mountain bike races (seasonal peaks). Stage races can often have an unexpected performance-boosting effect which cannot be produced by training alone.

Sitting Position on MTB and Road Bike

In order to be able to avoid or prevent possible orthopedic problems, it is important to adapt the sitting position of the racing bike to that of the mountain bike. And it is important to balance the sitting height, sitting distance (gap between the tip of the saddle and the center of the bottom bracket) and sitting length (distance between the tip of the saddle and the center of the handle bars). If possible, use the same saddle for both bikes and use only one shoe-pedal system. The common chain mountain bike chain length of 175 millimeters should also if possible be used on the racing bike.

Right from the start, it is important for the mountain biker to find the correct position on the MTB, which should then be transferred to the racing bike. Doing this the other way around would lead to a less comfortable position on the mountain bike which could jeopardize your performance potential.

Road races are good preparation.

When to train with the MTB and when with the road bike?
A simple rule of thumb is that road bikes should be used for long rides and spring training camps, while strength training and other specific workouts, particularly technique training, should be done on the mountain bike. However, it is up to the individual to decide how to train. Basically, if the same sitting position is used and if there are no crossover difficulties, all workouts are also possible with the MTB. However, if problems arise in the transfer from one bike to the other, you should not change too often and make sure that basic endurance, in particular, is always carried out on the racing bike. The reasons for the crossover difficulties should be investigated, though.

Compensatory training recovery workouts should also be performed on the racing bike, as such sessions on the MTB off-road are usually more intensive, and unwanted stress peaks are hard to avoid.

3.6　Training Errors

These are the most important training errors:
- Too intensive training, mainly in BE 1, BE 2, and in the race-specific zone, RSE. The emphasis should be on the development of a high aerobic capacity by means of BE 1.
- Over-intensive training during the week may prevent peak performance at the weekend. Symptoms are poor recovery (constant exhaustion) and empty glycogen reserves.
- Underestimation of work or education, and if training is not adapted accordingly, recovery can be inadequate.
- This can often be due to insufficient training in the BE 1 zone. Lack of periodization; mountain bikers have almost the same form throughout the year.
- Ignoring the laws of recovery.
- Excessive increases in workload and abrupt jumps in the yearly build-up, leading to performance stagnation or even deterioration.
- Not cutting down on training in the case of illness or infection, often leading to a loss of performance.
- Completely neglecting strength and strength endurance training.
- Poor cycling technique and no technique training.
- Diet is not adapted to the training type.
- Monotonous training, which often limits performance.
- Ignoring new training science discoveries.

This list is not exhaustive; the attentive trainer will be able to spot other errors.

3.7   Performance Categories

The training for the following performance categories is mainly intended for licensed riders. The training plans are for guidance only and must be adapted to the individual.

The races in the amateur categories without license are shorter.

Boys and Girls (U17)

The cross-country races for 15- and 16-year-olds last between 30 and 60 minutes, depending on the event. The girls' races tend to be shorter still. The short race duration means high intensity, but this doesn't mean training in this age group should be intensive.

The races in the boys and girls category are often dominated by the physically well-developed youngsters.

It is hard for the less physically developed boys and girls, particularly in the first group, to be successful in this age-group. While it is not uncommon for mountain bikers accustomed to success in this age group to have motivation problems due to lack of success in the senior men's or women's categories, the stragglers usually manage to make up the performance gap in this time. The slower riders can however compensate for weaker endurance and strength by above average technical skills, which may even give them the advantage in races.

Lots of Technique Training

Training for boys and girls should be as diverse as possible to provide a varied and flexible training structure. A wide-range of athletic training with the mountain bike as the focus should take precedence over any ambitions for success. This is not something to be avoided altogether though, just that the youngsters should be introduced to competitive sport in a measured and varied way. In a very technically demanding sport like mountain biking, technique training on the bike plays a key role in the overall training plan. Work on your bike coordination skills by playful training on the BMX bike, the track bike and the road bike (see, The Importance of Technique Training). There should still be an incomplete differentiation between downhill or cross-country, which is only explored later in the junior age group. This varied training allows basic coordination skills to be acquired and consolidated, thus forming the foundation for action and development reserves for later competitive and high-performance levels.

U17 Boys and Girls

Age	15 (m)	16 (m)	15 (f)	16 (f)
Annual training hours	250-350 hrs	350-450 hrs	200-300 hrs	300-400 hrs
Number of races	5-10	-15	5-10	-15
Max. BE 1 training duration	-4 hrs	-5 hrs	-3 hrs	-4 hrs
Training zones	BE 1, BE 2 RSE, ST	BE 1, BE 2, RSE, ST, SS (SE)	BE 1, BE 2, RSE, ST	BE 1, BE 2, RSE, ST, SS (SE)
Tips	• A lot of technique training	• Gentle SE and strength training from age 16	• Get used to greater traininig volumes	• Important to do a lot of cross-training

Weekly Cycle in PP and RP (Ages 15–16)

	PP II	RP
Monday	Stretching, exercises, strengthening exercises	Stretching, exercises, technique training strengthening exercises (30 min CT)
Thuesday	1 hr cross-training 1 hr gym-training	1-2 hrs BE 1 MTB or racing bike with ST intervals (3 x 2 min)
Wednesday	1-1,5 hrs cross-training	2-3 hrs BE 1 MTB or racing bike with ST tempo intervals (BE 2, RSE)
Thursday	Stretching, exercises	3 hrs BE 1 MTB or racing bike
Friday	2 hrs sports hall training	1 hr cross-training or rest day
Saturday	1-2 hrs BE 1 MTB or racing bike with technique training or cross-training	1 hr CT or BE 1 (technique training) or BE-Block, if no race
Sunday	2-3 hrs BE 1 MTB or racing bike (technique training)	Race or 2-4 hrs BE 1

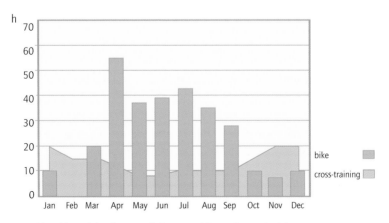

Monthly training hours split between bike and cross-training

The bike workouts should last between one and three hours, with the occasional, very long bike ride of four to five hours (with suitable training conditions and rests).

It should be left to the rider to choose which bike is preferred for endurance training. It would definitely be a mistake to force a youngster to do road training on the racing bike when they would really prefer to use their mountain bike.

Training for youngsters should be fun and as free from unnecessary pressures as possible.

They should also be encouraged to enter endurance races such as cross-country and road races, relay races, duathlons (with MTB) and triathlons.

As well as the daily stretching program, young bikers should also do functional strengthening exercises. There should not yet be specific training on weight machines, though, and, in any case, strength is already sufficiently trained by off-road biking.

In race planning for young bikers, make sure that they do not race too often to cut down the amount of time spent traveling. Ten to fifteen mountain bike races are quite enough, but this can be supplemented by a few races on the road if desired.

A one-week training camp or better still a training retreat during the holidays is recommended for youngsters, but they should be full of variety and avoid focusing on bike training on the road. This kind of training camp is an ideal opportunity to experiment with many different endurance activities that all contribute to the development of a basic endurance foundation. Trekking tours with climbing components or other adventure activities, partly based on adventure and experiential educational theory, are perfect for this. This can be a very exciting and enjoyable week for the young bikers, which allows them to train their basic endurance in many different ways.

Respect for nature should be taught at this age. Through a variety of experiences in and with nature, the young bikers learn to interact responsibly with nature. The aforementioned adventure activities are also great opportunities for personal and social education.

Juniors

Junior boys and girls aged 17 and 18 contest cross-country races lasting about 1 to 1.5 hours. The junior girls' races are slightly shorter like those for the girls in the previous age group. Many races are still won by precocious riders, although the disadvantage of the late developers does start to level out.

Training in this age group is characterized by increasingly specific training methods. While in the previous age group the emphasis is still on making endurance training fun, the focus now shifts gradually, depending on goals and motivation, to more performance-oriented training. This does not, however, mean that training should stop being fun!

Road training with the racing bike and the participation in road races is to be encouraged but is not strictly necessary.

Workouts last between two and four hours. However, occasionally extra-long workouts of five to six hours are necessary to develop endurance. Road training is recommended for these extra-long workouts. In a one- or two-week training camp, it is imperative that these long sessions be carried out on semi-flat terrain with low intensity.

Cross-Training

Cross-training is an essential part of mountain bike training that supplements training on the MTB or the racing bike. This means doing other endurance sports such as inline skating, trekking, cross-country skiing, running or orienteering. Cross-training particularly comes into its own in the preparation phases.

Alongside the ongoing functional strength training to avoid overuse injuries and muscular disbalances, targeted strength training is introduced in the junior age group. At first this involves doing bodyweight exercises and then after a while — as described in the chapter on strength training — using the gym and free weights.

One specific technique training session per week is necessary to perfect technical and coordination skills on the bike, with the emphasis on fun and variety.

In the junior age group, roughly 20 mountain bike races a year should be contested, which is hard to achieve for many bikers due to the low number of races available. It is also a good idea in this age group to diversify into road cycle racing and other endurance sports, particularly the duathlon and triathlon, cross-country running and orienteering, all of which greatly resemble the loading structure of a cross-country race, since, unlike in a road race, the athlete sets his own pace and performs according to his own physical and mental abilities.

Note that the intensity of endurance training in the junior age groups should be kept low. Juniors like to race against their training partners, so there is a danger that no basic endurance training is actually accomplished at all!

U19 Juniors

	17 (m)	18 (m)	17 (f)	18 (f)
Age	17 (m)	18 (m)	17 (f)	18 (f)
Annual training hours	400-550 hrs	500-650 hrs	350-450 hrs	400-550 hrs
Numbers of races	15-20	20-25	10-20	10-20
Max. BE 1 Training duration	-6 hrs	-7 hrs	-5 hrs	-6 hrs
Training zones	BE 1, BE 2, RSE, ST, SS, SE	BE 1, BE 2, RSE, ST, SS, SE	BE 1, BE 2, RSE, ST, SS, SE	BE 1, BE 2, RSE, ST, SS, SE
Tips	• SE and strength training are very important	• Get used to high volumes	• Enter road races	• A lot of cross-training

Weekly Cycle in PP and RP (Ages 17–18)

	PP II	RP
Monday	Stretching, exercises strengthening exercises	Stretching, exercises strengthening exercises (30 min CT)
Tuesday	1,5 hrs cross-training 1 hr strength or gym training	2 hrs BE 1 MTB or racing bike with SS-intervals (3 x 10 x 7 s) oder ST, SE
Wednesday	1,5-2 hrs cross-training	3 hrs BE 1 MTB or racing bike with tempo intervals (BE 2, RSE)
Thursday	Stretching, exercises, poss. 1 hr BE 1/2 MTB or racing bike	4-5 hrs BE 1 MTB or racing bike
Friday	2 hrs strength or gym training	Rest day
Saturday	2-3 hrs BE 1 MTB or racing bike with technique training or cross-training	1 hr CT or BE 1 (technique training) or BE-Block, if no race
Sunday	3-4 hrs BE 1 MTB or racing bike (technique training)	Race or 4-6 hrs BE 1

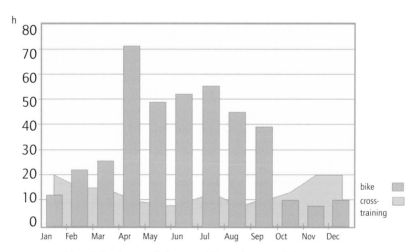

Monthly training hours split between bike and cross-training

Big fields require assertiveness, particularly at the start!

The junior age group is often the right time to decide between progressing to elite level or staying at regional level, without excluding the possibility of later development. Anyone who wants to make the jump to top international level must be prepared for the high-volume training required.

Many mountain bikers give up the sport at this age, as they are unwilling to put in the increasing training required and the racing speeds are way too fast for their capabilities. Luckily, there are also open races where the standard is slightly lower as far as most entrants are concerned.

Men

After the build-up and follow-up training phases, the next phase of high-performance training starts at the age of 19 for men, entailing very high training volumes and overall training workloads. This is not for everyone though, and for others, entry into the senior men's category coincides with a time when work or study commitments leave little free time for training, but they may still want to enter license races.

Men

Age	21 (m)	22 (m)	21 (m)	22 (m)
Annual training hours	600-700 hrs	700-800 hrs	800-900 hrs	900-1.000 hrs
Number of races	30-40	40-50	45-55	> 55
Max. BE 1 training duration	-8 hrs	-8 hrs	-8 hrs	-8 hrs
Training zones	BE 1, BE 2, RSE, ST, SS, SE	BE 1, BE 2, RSE, ST, SS, SE	BE 1, BE 2, RSE, ST, SS, SE	BE 1, BE 2, RSE, ST, SS, SE
Tips	• BE 1 and strength training are very important	• Highest volumes must be executed	• Take part in road races and poss. circuit races	• Continue with cross-training

Weekly Cycle in PP and RP (Ages 19-22)

	PP II	RP
Monday	Stretching, exercises strengthening exercises	Stretching, execises, technique training strengthening execises/1 hr CT
Tuesday	2,5 hrs cross-training 1 hr strength/gym training	3 hrs BE 1 MTB or racing bike with SS-intervals (3 x 12 x 7 s) oder ST, SE
Wednesday	2-3 hrs cross-training	4 hrs BE 1 MTB or racing bike with tempo intervals (BE 2, RSE)
Thursday	Stretching, exercises, poss. 2 hrs BE 1 MTB or racing bike	5-6 hrs BE 1 MTB or racing bike
Friday	2 hrs BE 1 MTB or racing bike (technique train.) or 1 hr strength/gym training	Rest day
Saturday	4 hrs BE 1 MTB or racing bike or cross-training	2 hrs CT/BE 1 (technique training) or BE block, if no race
Sunday	5-6 hrs BE 1 MTB or racing bike	Race or 6-8 hrs BE 1

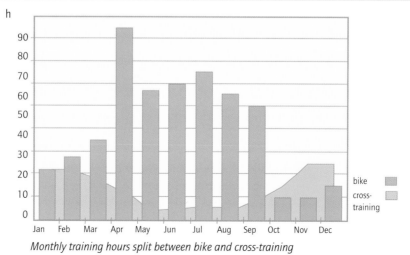

Monthly training hours split between bike and cross-training

However, many riders only come to the sport of mountain biking at this age, and their training needs are completely different.

Those riders on the high-performance pathway must now make sure that their training planning, execution and testing are as coordinated as possible in order to maximize training effectiveness. A description of a targeted training plan can be found in chapter 6.

Races in the men's category (licensed) last between one and three hours (apart from the marathon) and occasionally longer. Cross-country races usually last about two hours. Training in all zones increases to ensure continued development. The number of racing hours increases more than average compared to the overall number of hours, which reflects the increased importance of participation in road races. There is also the associated need for recovery training after each race, hence the slightly greater increase in **CT** zone training compared to the other zones. The importance of strength also increases in this category and must therefore be worked on more intensively.

The technical fundamentals should be mastered so that technique training is now focused on fine-tuning the techniques and mastering difficult techniques.

On or Off-Road?
By now, the required high volumes of **BE 1** zone training mean that it is harder and harder to meet them by riding only off-road on the mountain bike. Exercise intensity can be controlled more easily during road training, so road training is therefore an established component of the training program for mountain bikers. Participating in road races (circuit courses and genuine road races) also achieves the required number of racing hours, which otherwise would be very hard or impossible to do by competing only in mountain bike races. However, note that if you do try to complete all the necessary racing hours by only participating in mountain bike races (which involves driving around all over the place by car), you can easily end up overtraining, because the average intensity of a mountain bike race is considerably higher than that of a road race. More information on this problem can be found in the section, *MTB or Road Cycling?*

The sometimes very large starting fields, particularly in open races, mean that a secure riding technique and a fair amount of assertiveness are essential for success. The capacity for anaerobic mobilization should also be well-developed in order to have enough in reserve for the inevitable overtaking maneuvers.

Women

Alter	19 (f)	20 (f)	21 (f)	22 (f)
Annual training hours	500-600 hrs	600-700 hrs	700-800 hrs	800-900 hrs
Number of races	25-35	30-40	35-45	>45
Max. BE 1 training duration BE 1		-7 hrs	-7 hrs	-8 hrs
Training zones	BE 1, BE 2, RSE, ST, SS, SE	BE 1, BE 2, RSE, ST, SS, SE	BE 1, BE 2, RSE, ST, SS, SE	BE 1,BE 2, RSE, ST, SS, SE
Tips	• BE 1, SE and strengthening training very important	• Highest volumes must be executed	• Take part in road and poss. circuit races	• Continue with cross-training

Weekly Cycle in PP and RP (Ages 19-22)

	PP II	RP
Monday	Stretching, exercises strengthening exercises	Stretching, execises, technique training strengthening execises/1 hr CT
Tuesday	1 hr cross-training 1 hr strength/gym training	2 hrs BE 1 MTB or racing bike with SS-intervals (2 x 10 x 7 s) or ST, SE
Wednesday	1-2 hrs cross-training	3 hrs BE 1 MTB or racing bike with tempo intervals (BE 2, RSE)
Thursday	Stretching, exercises (technique train.), poss. 2 hrs BE 1 MTB or racing bike	4-5 hrs BE 1 MTB or racing bike
Friday	1 hr BE 1 MTB or racing bike 2 hrs strength/gym training	Rest day
Saturday	3 hrs BE 1 MTB or racing bike or cross-training	1 hr CT or BE 1 (technique training) or BE-Block, if no race
Sunday	4-5 hrs BE 1 MTB or racing bike	Race or 5-7 hrs BE 1

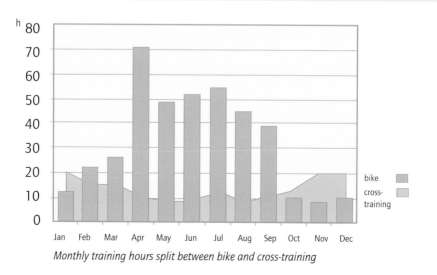

Monthly training hours split between bike and cross-training

Women

Women's cross-country races usually last between one and two hours. The fields in races below the big international races (World Cup) are usually really small and diverse in terms of performance level.

The greatest areas of weakness in women's mountain biking are inadequate basic endurance, poor to average strength and weak technique. It is therefore important to focus on improving these areas in training.
Apart from these characteristics, the same principles apply to women's training as to men's.

When training with men, it is important for women to find a training group that corresponds to their performance level. However, it is often the case that women train with men who are at a higher performance level than themselves, so that they train outside the planned intensity zones and training does not have the desired effect. The same is also true for the junior girls age groups and for novice cyclists.

Diet and nutrition are discussed in chapter 7, Nutrition.

Targeted and Intensive Technique Training

Intensive technique training must be carried out in the women's age group. Often, due to their upbringing, girls and women increasingly lack technical coordination skills on the mountain bike compared to boys or men of the same age.

In all age groups, there is a noticeable tendency for many bikers with outstanding performance test results but inadequate riding technique to waste time in starts and tricky sections which cannot be made up on the climbs and flat sections. This is yet another reminder of the need for training to be as diverse as possible in this very technically demanding sport.

Fitnessbiker: Beginner

Annual training hours	150-200 hrs	200-250 hrs	200-300 hrs
Max. BE 1 training duration	-3 hrs	-4 hrs	-5 hrs
Training zones	BE 1, BE 2, RSE	BE 1, BE 2, RSE	BE 1, BE 2, RSE
Tips	• Health Check-up • Also do long workouts	• Important to do compensation sports, cross-training	• Compensation exercises important

Weekly Cycle in PP und RP (200 - 250 hrs)

	PP II	RP
Montag	–	–
Dienstag	30 min cross-training or 45 min BE 1 MTB	1 hr BE 1 MTB or cross-training
Mittwoch	1hr BE 1/2 MTB or in cross-training	1-2 hrs BE 1 mit BE 2/RSE-intervals MTB
Donnerstag	Stretching, exercises, strengthening exercises	Stretching, exercises, strengthening exercises
Freitag	–	–
Samstag	1,5 hrs BE 1 MTB with technique training	1-2 hrs BE 1 with technique training
Sonntag	2 hrs BE 1 MTB	2-3 hrs BE 1 MTB or cyclosportive or gran fondo

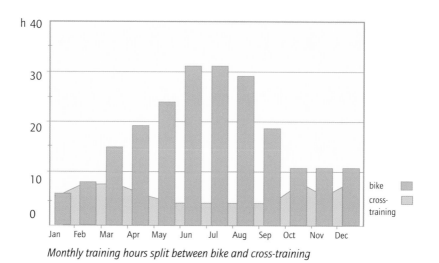

Monthly training hours split between bike and cross-training

Seniors

In the senior licensed category, races will be mastered by former top amateurs, who often also have cross-country experience and are almost unbeatable due not only to their technical abilities but also to their strength endurance. This is particularly true in comparison to beginners, who have cut their competitive teeth in open races.

The senior category can therefore be subdivided into two groups. This division could be made in every age group, but merits particular attention in the senior category as the differences are so great.

As well as the above-mentioned riders who may have more than three decades of cycling experience, riders who may have gained endurance experience in other sports and others who have no previous sporting experience at all come to the sport of mountain bike racing and take part in license races. It would be hard to find more disparate opponents!

The experienced rider should train in the same way as the men in the previous category, but they often have a radically reduced timeframe. Targeted strength training is also recommended in this category but is often neglected as the rider may already have good strength and strength endurance due to his many years of racing experience. Long basic endurance workouts are absolutely vital and should, if possible, be performed at least once every two weeks to maintain basic endurance levels.

Functional Exercises

Particularly in the senior age groups, the importance of targeted functional strengthening exercises increases greatly in order to compensate for postural damage and overuse from years of cycling. A daily stretching program is also a must for senior mountain bikers.

Beginners and Fitness Bikers

The beginner must first concentrate on basic endurance training to create a foundation on which to build more specific training. So the majority of training time is spent on developing basic endurance, which can easily be done by including cross-training. The emphasis should, however, be on bike training so that any technical deficits may be corrected. If endurance ability is not adequate, the intensity zone used in races will be too high. This also negatively impacts the riding technique because of the very high stress placed on the rider.

Specific technique training, ideally with experienced riders, must be carried out twice a week.

Marathon

Annual training hours	200-400 hrs	400-600 hrs	600-800 hrs
Max. BE 1 training duration	-6 hrs	-7 hrs	-8 hrs
Training zones	BE 1, BE 2, RSE, SE	BE 1, BE 2, RSE, SE	BE 1, BE 2, RSE, SE
Tips	• A lot of technique training • Oft lange Einheiten	• Important to do compensation sports, cross-training	• Compensation exercises important

Weekly Cycle in PP and RWP (400-600 hrs)

	VP II	WP
Monday	Stretching, exercises, strengthening exercises	Stretching, exercises strengthening exercises
Tuesday	1 hr cross-training or 45 min BE 1 MTB	1,5-2,5 hrs BE 1 MTB or racing bike 15 min SE or cross-training
Wednesday	1,5-2 h GA 1 MTB/Rennrad oder 1,5-2 h Crosstraining	1-2 hr BE 1 with BE 2/RSE-intervals with MTB or racing bike
Thursday	Stretching, exercises, strengthening exercises	2-3 hrs BE 1 MTB or racing bike
Friday	1 hr cross-training	1 hr CT/BE 1 MTB (technique training) or rest
Saturday	1-2 hrs BE 1 MTB or racing bike (technique training)	3-5 hrs BE 1 mit MTB or racing bike
Sunday	3-4 hrs BE 1 MTB or racing bike	4-6 hrs BE 1 MTB or racing bike or marathon

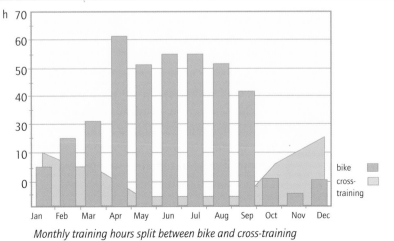

Monthly training hours split between bike and cross-training

Beginners should also focus on strength training both with the bike and in the gym, making functional strengthening exercises and stretching an integral part of their program.

Those who find it hardest are definitely those who have no endurance sports experience at all. It takes a good two years of training to achieve the physical adaptations necessary for a good level of basic endurance, which in turn requires a great deal of will power and determination.

Before starting mountain bike training, get a thorough check-up by a sports doctor to eliminate any possible health risks from the start. At first beginners should train in moderation, paying attention to how their bodies feel so as to avoid overuse or injury.

The main training zones are therefore only **BE 1** and **2** and **RSE**. Specific, high-intensity and target-oriented training are out of the question for fitness bikers or beginners. In order to raise general training capacity, beginners and fitness bikers should do regular cross-training. Strength training is not necessary but compensation exercise and stretching are.

Marathon Bikers

More and more bikers are taking part in marathons, with a wide range of performance levels and goals. The marathon is a kind of hybrid between racing and touring events.

Irrespective of goals, however, it is essential for all marathon bikers to perform long training sessions. Long and overlong **BE 1** workouts must be trained in blocks in the preparation for marathons. Only a well-developed aerobic foundation with a functional fat metabolism can provide the energy supply for the duration of a marathon distance (often up to six hours). Speed and speed strength training take a back seat due to the length of the race, but strength endurance is important.

Through targeted technique training, the marathon biker can create biking technique reserves that will protect him in the last third of the marathon from potentially serious riding errors in a very fatigued state.

The illustration shows different volumes for three groups of marathon bikers. The first group only has a basic workload and prepares in the last eight weeks before the big day with high training volumes to cope with the distance.

In the second group and above all the third groups with a high training workload, the focus is increasingly on performance, hence the higher training volumes and intensities required that are performed all year. This total training amount, spread throughout the year, forms the foundation for a higher average tempo and prepares the rider to cope with at least brief bursts of speed.

Food and beverage intake is vital for marathons and must be practiced in training rides in order to avoid problems with new foods and drinks during a race.

3.8   Training Camps

Positioning Training Camps in the Annual Plan
Anyone planning a training camp should start thinking before the start of the training year, ideally in the transition phase, about the timing of the camp and which part of the training year build-up it is most suited to.

If the training year is broken down using chapter 4.1, Periodization, as an example, then it makes most sense to schedule the training camp at the end of preparation phase II or at the start of preparation phase III. The aim of a training camp at this time should be to improve basic endurance, and, if there is enough time, to carry out long and extra-long workouts in the **BE** zones. There is also the possibility of compensating for such high volumes in the training camp with suitable recovery methods such as stretching or physiotherapy, but most of all, with adequate sleep.

Training camps for young bikers should take place during the spring school holidays, which correspond with the end of **PP III**. In **PP III**, normally specific content is trained, as basic endurance already should be very well-developed by this stage. If good winter weather means that sufficient basic endurance has been trained in **PP I** and **PP II**, or the desired level has already been reached, then in a training camp in **PP III**, quite intensive training forms can be used, while also slightly reducing training volume. However, for the aforementioned reasons, the emphasis should still be on the formation or consolidation of basic endurance. More intensive training forms should, at most, be used in the second training week, after using two **BE I** blocks for acclimatization in the first week, for example. In the second week the volume would then be reduced a little and broken up with more intensive intervals (**BE 2**, **RSE**).

As well as the spring or foundation training camp, camps can also take place during the racing phase. For youngsters, the summer holidays are ideal, while adults can fit theirs in around their other activities.

Preparation

In any case, a training camp should be prepared for and followed up following training methodology. The preparation and follow-up has been described previously in the chapter on periodization in the **PP III** section.

Several build-up and load preparation microcycles (weeks) should be scheduled to allow time for just one recovery week immediately before the training camp. After the training camp, also schedule a few days to a week of recovery. Before a foundation training camp, the ambitious mountain biker (men's category) should have completed at least 1,500 kilometers or 60 hours on the bike. A lower limit for hobby and junior riders is roughly 800–1,000 kilometers or 30–40 hours. These figures relate to the **PP II** period starting in January.

Training Camp Timeframe

Ideally, a foundation training camp should last two weeks, while one week is enough for a summer training camp. One week is also the right length for young bikers, but this can be extended to two weeks as long as the program is varied.

Training Camp Location

If you aim for a Spring training camp, take a look at possibilities to go to California, Colorado or other States in the US where the weather is faily mild around that time of the year. In Europe Spain, the south of France and Majorca are good locations.

Ensure that three to five bike rollers are available at the training camp venue, which the riders can use to train on bad weather days. Two workouts on the rollers (morning, afternoon) and games and circuit training in the gym are a good substitute for a missed road workout and also provide variety.

The one-week training camp can easily be conducted close by. You need a low mountain range where you can find a change of scene with beautiful countryside and also ideal terrain for mountain biking.
One effect of the increasing professionalization of the sport is that more and more riders are performing training camps at high altitude in order to acquire physiological advantages over other bikers.

Fig. 3.27: Spring training camp for the men's category (14 days, volume-oriented)

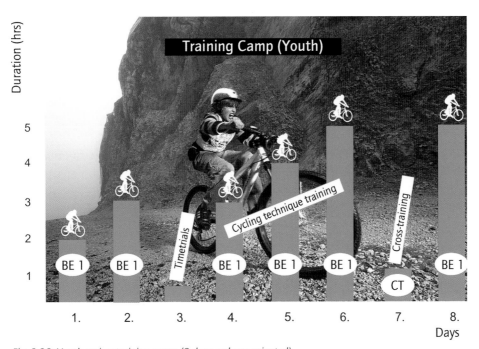

Fig. 3.28: Youth spring training camp (8 days, volume-oriented)

Which Bike for Training Camp?

In a foundation training camp, it doesn't matter in principle whether you train on a mountain bike with slicks or a racing bike. However, training on the road is important in order to maintain a balanced loading intensity. When riding off-road, it is very hard to maintain an even intensity in the **BE 1** zone due to the rough cycling surfaces and different types of terrain. Experience has shown that even mixed groups of riders (men and women) can train together on mountain bikes with slicks and racing bikes, as long as they are of similar ability.

However, in specific training camps, it is necessary to train on mountain bikes off-road, because this training must be sport-specific. If high training volumes on the bike are required, keep the intensity low. If the emphasis is on basic endurance, for maintenance purposes for example, it is best to train on the road, and the type of bike doesn't matter.

Training Camp Structure

A two-week basic training camp is, like the microcycles, divided into separate blocks. The 14 days are split into two-, three- or four-day blocks with one recovery day between the blocks when a short **CT** ride is performed.

For youngsters, two- and three-day blocks are very beneficial, and at high performance levels, four-day blocks can also be used, which are both physically and mentally demanding.

Each block is structured so it increases in difficulty each day. During a training camp, the volume of each block also increases. The block formation works because it ensures a gradual increase in workload, and it also ensures that there are enough recovery phases. There is a defined, easily understandable workload to mentally prepare for. The first day of a block is usually relatively easy to cope with; on the second day, motivational problems and physical aches and pains start to appear, and on the third day when training is hardest, the rider can look forward to the recovery day the following day.

Lower-ability bikers and those lacking in motivation may have problems with motivation and over-exertion using the four-day block structure, so the last and hardest workout may be cut short. By reversing the training order within a block, the high motivational and rested state after the recovery day enable the very high-volume workout to be performed with ease. The next two days follow with reduced training volumes.

In blocks where the training difficulty increases every day, there is an accumulation of fatigue, and in the reversed block arrangement, the decrease in training stimulus size means that the fatigue level is roughly even after the first day. This second method is mentally easier to cope with. This reversed block should not be used as the first block of a training camp though, which is intended for familiarization and acclimatization purposes.

Training Intensity

It is important to adhere to basic endurance training intensity in training camps, because excessive intensity combined with high volumes leads to a significant recovery deficit. Often, mountain bikers do not stick to these intensity guidelines and ride inclines, in particular, too hard. This causes a training deficit that cannot be made up during the training camp. Instead, the deficit is increased as more training is performed so that even weeks after the training camp, the negative consequences of the excessive intensity are still present in the form of reduced performance ability. Training at a low intensity usually enables a noticeable improvement in form from block to block, and this improvement should be tested in the last block. On one day, find a mountain or another course for speed riding where you can ride flat-out for a few miles. A time-trial can also add interest to the training camp and relieve the monotony of basic endurance training. With such low intensity training, there is no risk of injury, and, above all, the pressure to ride fast and test yourself can be controlled.

Riders should cycle in pairs or in groups of no more than 12. It is easy to ride at basic intensities, even on hilly terrain, as long as the correct gear ratio is selected. For example, gear ratios of 39/23 or even 25 are required to be able to handle even steep inclines in the **BE 1** zone.

3.9   SRM PowerMeter: High-Tech Training

Following is a short section on SRM training system that has revolutionized scientific research in the sport of cycling in general, including mountain biking.

In the early years of performance testing, despite the recognized connection between physiological loading parameters such as heart rate, lactate concentration and oxygen uptake on the one hand and physical performance on the other, it wasn't possible to put the knowledge acquired in the laboratory into practice due to a lack of measuring equipment. So the compromise was to use the heart rate as a control parameter to measure power and specific metabolic states determined by lactate measurements. This was done without knowing whether the values obtained in the lab actually corresponded to those data obtained on- or off-road on your bike.

For the past 25 years, the SRM training system has enabled a sensitive electronic sensor (strain gage) installed in the bike crank to accurately measure power on the racing and mountain bike. The measurements are transferred telemetrically (i.e., wirelessly) to a central processing unit located on the handlebar where all the parameters are displayed. The microship is capable of storing over many hours (130 hrs with 1 sec storing interval). The measured data (e.g., power, heart rate, speed, cadence, time, distance and altitude) is continually stored at a pre-set time interval (0.5–5 sec). For example, data is transmitted and stored every five seconds. After a workout or race, the data can be downloaded to a computer using a USB cable with the appropriate software where it can be displayed and analyzed.

The graphics and statistical evaluation of the data enable detailed conclusions to be drawn about the rider's performance development. In addition, the system enables optimal intensity management during exercise, because it allows power to be used as a control parameter along with heart rate.

By providing accurate performance testing to establish the intensity zones, the SRM system allows elite mountain bikers to train efficiently.

SRM
PowerMeter

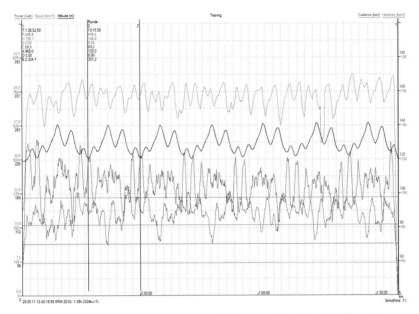

Fig. 3.29: Parameters during a Cross-Country World Cup race (Location: Offenburg, Germany; leader: Wolfram Kurschat, 72 kg, Topeak Ergon Racing Team; date: 05-29-2011; smoothing 1%)

However, it is very hard for the interested layperson to make full use of the SRM training system, as comprehensive scientific knowledge and a lot of experience is necessary to use the equipment effectively and interpret the results.

A few performance testing institutes now offer intensive training support using power meters.

Analysis of Racing Effort

The detailed analysis of mountain bike races using SRM system evaluation is extremely interesting, as it reveals a performance structure that even confuses many experts. A detailed explanation of this would exceed the scope of this book, and an introduction has already been given in chapter 2.

Example: Cross-Country

At first glance, many interesting details can be identified relating to the cross-country race effort when viewing figure 3.29. It shows the Cross-Country World Cup race in Offenburg, Germany (2011). The rider Wolfram Kurschat of the team Topeak-Ergon took 31st place, 5 min 39 sec behind the leader.

The **heart rate** (red) lies between 145 and 170 bpm with a core area between 160 and 165. The time elapsed between peak heart rate and peak power (green) is around 40–60 sec.

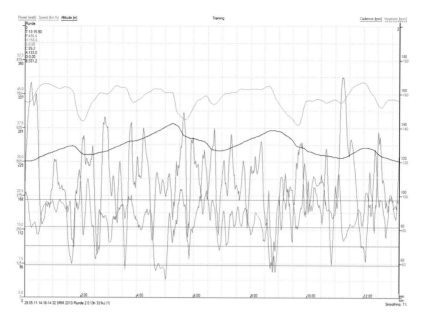

Fig. 3.30: Parameters of a circuit in a Cross-Country World Cup rate (Location: Offenburg, Germany; rider: Wolfram Kurschat, 72 kg, Topeak-Ergon Racing Team; date: 05-29-2011; no smoothing)

The circulation therefore has a delayed reaction to effort, because the power is first provided anaerobically and then the energy deficit in the aerobic–anaerobic transition area must be covered by an increased oxygen uptake. Likewise, **the altitude profile** (black) and the resulting power profile of the circuit in Offenburg can be seen very clearly.

The average **power** of 405 Watts (green) over the analyzed period of 1:35 minutes is very high, but more important are the effort spikes (over 800 W), which are not very clear in these smoothed curves. What is clear, though, is that the power curve shows a wide oscillation between very high and very low values. This power oscillation is typical for cross-country mountain bike races and is what distinguishes them from longer road races. Only on flat and technically simple courses do you find longer sections with even power. On normal courses, the power varies significantly due to the frequent freewheeling sections, accelerations and climbs. This situation should be reflected in the training methodology with reinforced strength and speed strength training.

In this respect, the behavior of the velocity curve is interesting, as it is usually a mirror image of the power curve so that where the power curve value is lowest, the **speed** is usually highest. These are downhill freewheeling sections, as the cadence is also zero. The speed is not given in the curve shown here for reasons of clarity.

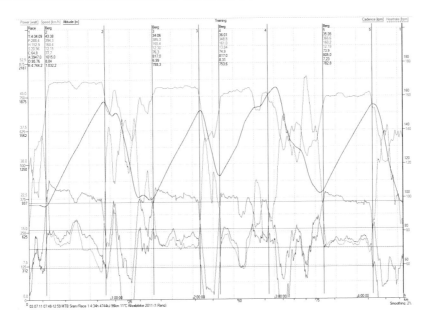

Fig. 3.31: Graph showing the parameters of a marathon (Location: Brixental, Germany; rider: Alban Laka-ta, 76 kg, Topeak-Ergon Racing Team; date: 07-03-2011; smoothing 2%).

The **average cadence** (blue curve) is 88 rpm. The highest cadence peaks are 130, and the average peaks are 100. Wolfram Kurschat, the cyclist, has a rather unusually high cadence for a mountain biker. The importance of strength endurance training in mountain biking at low cadence is underestimated. In the numerous acceleration phases, especially, high levels of strength are very important. Working on speed and developing high cadence is important in order to reach a high cadence and maintain it on flatter sections and for acceleration purposes.

Figure 3.30 shows the parameters of Wolfram Kurschat during a circuit without data smoothing. The wide oscillations are immediately obvious. The power reaches an average of 416 Watts with 10 spikes above 800 Watt in 13 minutes. Within this short timeframe, the rider has to briefly generate 600 Watts or more about 40 times. This illustrates the importance of strength and anaerobic mobilization.

Example: Marathon

Figures 3.31 and 3.32 show the data profile during the Kitzalpmarathon of Alban Lataka, who as recent World Champion went on to win the marathon. Unlike a cross-country race, in a marathon the very smooth curves of all parameters are immediately obvious.

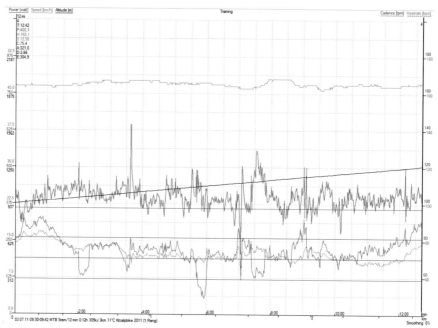

Fig. 3.32: Parameters during a long uphill section (12 min on mountain 2) during the Kitzalpmarathon (Location: Kitzbühel; rider: Alban Lakata, 76 kg, Topeak-Ergon Racing Team; date: 07-03-2011; no smoothing).

Heart rate (red) and power (green) are primarily affected by the altitude profile (black). In the four long climbs lasting between 34 to 43 minutes, Alban rides between 350 and 395 Watts on average, and the heart rate oscillates between 160 and 168. The cadence falls in the course of the four mountains from 78 to 74 rpm. In particular in figure 3.32 (without smoothing), the even effort distribution on the mountain is striking, that is it is only interrupted by the course geography (curves) or tactical events. In marathons in low mountain ranges, the parameter curve is subject to significantly more frequent changes due to the frequently changing profile. Nevertheless, the effort during each phase is again very even.

In combination with performance testing research and corresponding race and training data analysis, a rider can in long, even sections manage his threshold performance very accurately and avoid over- or under-loading.

In comparison to a cross-country race, it is obvious that because of the very different demands (e.g., race length and parameter fluctuations), specialists in each discipline must train very differently. Intervals and short accelerations, strength training and technique training are more important for a cross-country rider than for a marathon specialist who must be able to cope with races lasting twice as long.

Wolfram Kurschat during the 2011
Cross-Country World Cup in Offenburg

Alban Lakata during the 2011
Kitzalp Marathon

4   Strength Training for Mountain Bikers

According to the mountain biking requirement profile described in chapter 2, strength is second in importance only to endurance for overall performance. Good strength endurance capacity is increasingly necessary to be able to compete at the highest level, which again illustrates the special importance of strength training.

Although endurance levels in mountain biking still lag behind those in road cycling, and so there is still room for improvement in the building up training and loading reserves, all types of strength must also be worked on for the rider to fulfill his performance potential. If two riders have the same endurance capacity, the one with higher strength levels will be capable of riding with a higher gear ratio to obtain greater propulsive power. The result is a higher velocity or, if the speed remains the same, reduced metabolic stress.

Strength training can either be done in the weight room or gym with your own bodyweight, free weights or machines or by training on the mountain bike itself. When performed on the mountain bike or racing bike, strength training becomes specific strength training, and the former training becomes nonspecific strength training.

Strength training also includes functional strengthening exercises for both injury prevention and rehab purposes and can also be used specifically to develop a more economical pedaling action.

Avoid Excessive Muscle Development

It is important to note that the type of strength required by mountain bikers absolutely does not involve increasing muscle mass, just improving the training condition of the muscles.

This functional improvement is achieved by developing maximum strength and coordination within a muscle as well as between each muscle involved in a particular action (i.e., intra- and inter-muscular coordination). Long-term, frequent training with heavy to maximum weight is required to produce a clear increase in the cross-sectional area (muscle growth). Although this is not desirable, as it reduces endurance, increases the amount of muscle mass to be supplied with oxygen and also increases the bodyweight.

Muscle Anatomy

Motor neurons (nerve cells) in the spinal column cause the individual muscle fibers to contract. A motor neuron and its muscle fiber are called a motor unit. If a motor neuron in the spinal column is stimulated by the brain, it transmits this information and causes all the muscle fibers it serves to contract. The amount of strength is determined by the number of motor neurons involved.

A strength training program teaches the body to voluntarily recruit as many of these motor neurons as possible in order to maximize the theoretical strength potential (number of available muscle fibers). A certain area always remains autonomous though (i.e., protected for dangerous situations). Intramuscular training increases the number of muscle fibers voluntarily taking part in a contraction. The muscles important for strength training and their actions are explained in chapter 2.

The Importance of Strength Training

Training science is still not completely unanimous about how to train, although very good results can be obtained using traditional methods. A particular area of disagreement is the definition of the individual strength types and how to train them, as different research teams sometimes put forward absolutely contradictory opinions.

The methods and exercises presented here correspond mainly to traditional theories. According to newer findings, maximum strength has a much greater importance for the level of the other strength types (e.g., speed strength, strength endurance, explosive strength) than had been previously thought, which particularly affects mountain biking due to its high strength component. Strength training is definitely more important in mountain biking than in road cycling.

When to Train

It often happens that a biker's hard-won strength reverts back to starting levels during the racing season as it is not maintained. All it takes is a regular, once-weekly strength workout to maintain these strength levels and even improve your performance on the bike.

So, it is advisable to ride a few miles less every week and use that time for strength training. One hour is sufficient, for example on a Tuesday, Wednesday or Thursday, before or after an easy endurance workout. Bad weather days are also ideal times to slot in a strength training workout. Determining which day of the microcycle the strength training should be carried out depends on the racing schedule, though. For example, if you are racing on a Saturday or Sunday, never do a strength workout on a Thursday.

4.1 Periodization

Like endurance training, strength training also uses periodization. Different cycles with different loads and training methods should prepare the biker for a seasonal peak. For bikers without real peak goals, periodization aids long-term performance improvement and the optimal preparation for the racing phase.

The strength foundation is always laid in the preparation phase in the weight room or the gym. To maintain a basic level of strength, strengthening exercises are performed several times a week. The subsequent periodization nevertheless involves training in the weight room on machines and with free weights. This strength periodization is based on a single-peak racing phase in the summer. If there are two racing phases (e.g., summer and winter), each phase is shortened accordingly. During the long racing phase, training must, of course, be varied. Single strength workouts or strength endurance workouts with average loads and maximum repetitions provide variety both mentally and in terms of training methodology. Such intensive workouts should not be performed if recovery is not complete. Strength workouts lasting 45–60 minutes are enough to maintain your acquired strength during the racing season, enabling you to ride more effectively and to cope with the high gear ratios that are essential for a high performance level.

1. Preparation phase I (familiarization phase)
In November, the muscles are initially trained with low loads (45–55% and high numbers of repetitions, 15–20) and 2–4 sets and prepared for the next more intensive training. Train two to three times per week in the weight room during this phase. Before and after this phase, perform a maximum strength test to calculate weights.

2. Preparation phase II (growth phase)
In December and January, the muscles are loaded with 60–70% of maximum strength, and 3–4 sets of 8–12 reps carried out. If training is only done twice a week, there is no danger of the muscles being overdeveloped.

3. Preparation phase III (maximum strength phase)
February is used for improving maximum strength. Training is done with very heavy weights at 80–100% and only 4–6 sets of 1–5 reps, which improves both maximum strength and speed strength.

	Intensity	Reps	Sets	Sessions/Week
PP I	45-55 %	15-20	2-4	2-3
PP II	60-70 %	8-12	3-4	2-3
PP III	80-100 %	1-5	4-6	2-3
RP	60-70 %	8	3	1-2
TP	–	–	–	–

Fig. 4.1: Annual strength training program for mountain bikers

Strength training should be done two to three times per week. Maximum strength capacity should be checked several times during this phase and the weights adjusted accordingly. In March, training is similar to that in **PP II**. During the spring training camp and the recovery days that precede and follow it in March, avoid weight training but still continue functional strengthening exercises.

4. Racing phase (strength maintenance phase)
In the racing phase from April onward, strength capacity must be maintained by performing 3 sets of 8 reps at 60–70% max load once or twice per week. During the long racing phase, the strength training load must be cycled and varied, just like the endurance load (e.g., by occasionally doing a maximum strength workout, reducing training after a tough race and also varying the exercises). Strength training should also be adapted for the most intensive training phase before the seasonal peak. Workouts should be more frequent and higher intensity, as in maximum strength training.

5. Transition phase (strength loss phase)
In the transition phase, as described in the previous chapter, training is no longer as focused. There should be no weight training at all in this phase to allow strength levels to drop in order to be raised again during the course of the following training year. Strengthening exercises should be continued, though.

At grass-roots and keep-fit sports level, strength training is reduced to low weights and high reps (phase I, possibly II).

4.2 Strength Training Rules

As strength training is usually very stressful for the body and incorrect movement can do a great deal of damage, a few training rules and the correct movement execution must be kept in mind.

- An intensive warm-up program must precede strength training, whatever form it takes. The higher the load, the longer the warm-up program should be.
- Correct and clean movement execution is essential (concentrate on the exercise).
- Keep your back straight; do not lift weights with a curved back.
- If possible when working with free weights, work with a partner for safety reasons.
- Breathe gently during the exercises, no forced exhalation.
- When training on machines, set them up to accommodate your body size and weight exactly.
- Joints should only be loaded along their physiological movement axes; evasive movements can cause damage.
- Do not strain the ends of joints.
- Just like endurance training, strength training follows the principle of gradual loading increase; only once a basic strength foundation has been developed can maximum strength training begin.
- Like in endurance training, the load must be varied and cycled, as constantly training with the same load fails to trigger an adaptation process or associated training effect.
- Strength training must be performed regularly (1-3 times per wk).
- Strength training must be adapted to performance level and age; before the age of 15, strength training should be limited to bodyweight exercises, and overloading must be avoided.
- Remember the importance of recovery (i.e., don't train when the body is exhausted after a race or hard workout); allow two to four minutes rest between sets.
- Do not perform strength training after an intensive workout.
- A short bike ride with a few accelerations (e.g., in the special strength area) achieves a positive transfer effect of strength training into the cyclical pedaling action.
- Strength training shortens the muscles, so a thorough stretching program must be carried out afterward.

4.3 Strength Training in Practice

No specific numbers of reps and sets are given for the strength training exercises suggested below, as every athlete is different; instead, choose the best reps and sets for you from the training zones based on your training experience.

4.3.1 Weight Room

Following is a weight training program that covers the entire training year, with two strength circuits shown as examples. The terms *series* or *set* and *repetition* are explained in chapter 3.

Determine Maximum Strength

The loading intensity is given as a percentage of maximum strength, which—after a thorough warm-up—must be tested on each machine or for each exercise separately in order to calculate the percentages for the respective loads. In a maximum strength test, take three or four attempts at your maximum weight. Make a note of the figures and use them to calculate your training program, and put it down in writing. A maximum test should be repeated every four to six weeks in order to adapt loading to your changing strength levels. An intensive warm-up program is extremely important before lifting these maximum loads.

Exercises for Different Muscle Groups

The numbers following the muscle groups relate to the anatomical diagrams of the muscles on pages 23–26 and are used instead of the muscle names. The numbers underneath the exercises refer to the strength training exercises described in the next section.

Leg muscles

- **Knee extensor 25, 26, 31**
  Exercises: different leg presses; squats with barbell, not too deep; jumps
  1, 2, 3

- **Knee flexor 36, 38, 39**
  Exercises: different pulling machines; flexor machine
  4
  Work with different knee angles to simulate the pedaling cycle. Also perform some sets with lighter weights and smaller angles (i.e., greater flexion) in order to make the acquired strength usable on the mountain bike.

- **Lower leg muscles** 32, 33, 34, 39, 44
  Exercises: calf raise machine; calf raises with barbell; foot raises
  5, 6

- **Hip flexor** 24, 27, 30 also 25, 26, 31 Exercises: leg press machine (also used to train hip flexors); specific hip flexor machines
  4

- **Hip extensor** 36, 40, 42
  Exercises: leg press; squats with barbell
  1, 2, 3

Arm and shoulder muscles

- **Biceps** 19, 20, 21 (11)
  Exercises: biceps curls; lying pull-down; lat pull machine; chin-ups
  7, 8, 10

- **Triceps** 15, 16
  Exercises: triceps curls; push-ups
  9

- **Chest muscles** 4
  Exercises: bench press, regular and incline
  9

- **Forearm muscles** 17, 22, 23
  Exercises: wrist curls
  11
  Handling free weights also train the forearm muscles. A hand press can also be used for training.

Core muscles

- **Back muscles** 3, 12
  Exercises: back machine or weights; push-ups; see chapter 5, Functional Stretching
  12

- **Abdominal muscles** 6, 7, 8
  Exercises: crunches; abs machine; abdominal exercises in stretching chapter; push-ups

The core muscles are strengthened in all exercises with free weights, which is why training with free weights is preferable. Functional strengthening exercises using one's own bodyweight are particularly good for working on the abdominal and back muscles.

Exercise Selection

1 Leg press
The leg press must first be done with a knee angle of about 70–80 degrees, and then different angles can be used. In the extension phase, do not fully straighten the knee, because there is a danger of overloading. With heavy weights, make sure the movement execution is slow and controlled; with light weights, an explosive extension is possible. Train the calf muscles by using light weights and placing only the balls of the feet on the foot pad and actively extending the ankles.

2 Squats with barbell
The barbell is supported by the arms and the upper back. The toes point outward slightly and the heels can rest on a block to offload the Achilles tendons. It is important to maintain muscle tension in the upper body and to control knee extension and flexion. The back must be kept straight. To learn the correct technique, practice with light weights and seek guidance from an experienced lifter. Perform both squats up to a 90-degree knee angle and very deep squats.

Squat jumps

3 Squat jumps
Take off from both feet, keeping the back straight. After landing on flat feet or, better still, the balls of the feet, bend the knees to no more than 70 degrees, and spring back up as fast as possible. Perform 3–5 sets of 10–30 reps. This exercise is a particularly good way of improving climbing and sprinting ability. At elite level, the difficulty can be increased by jumping down from and back up to low benches. Also, one-leg step-ups and jumps down from boxes are also suitable. Increase loading only very gradually.

4 Leg curls and leg pulley machine

The leg curl machine makes it possible to isolate and strength the hamstrings. Do not rest the kneecap on the bench, and align the pivot of the knee with the pivot of the machine. The hips and the abdomen must be tensed.

It is better to train on the pulley machine, where several joints can be worked at once. By leaning the upper body slightly forward, the ankle with the cuff can be actively extended backward and carefully brought forward to bend the leg. This also works the hip flexors. This exercise can also be performed with a Thera-Band®.

Calf raise

5 Calf raise

Calf raises are performed to strengthen the calf muscles in isolation. Facing the wall, stand on the balls of the feet, extend the ankle and then sink back down. The other foot is either suspended in the air or rested on the heel of the active leg. It is important to extend the knee of the active leg so that only the calf muscles perform the raising and lowering actions. This exercise is even more effective on a step, the top of a gym horse or other object. Perform 2–4 sets of 15–50 reps on each leg.

6 Foot flexion

Attach the Thera-Band® to a wallbar. Sit on the floor, ideally without shoes to avoid wear and tear on the Thera-Band®. With the leg extended, place your foot in the loop of the Thera-Band®. Now pull both toes toward you and then relax them again. Thera-Bands® are available in different strengths. It is also possible to do this exercise as a pair activity

7 Biceps curls

Biceps curls are performed by a supported free arm with a dumbbell in a sitting position. The back should be kept as straight as possible.

8 Lat pull machine

The multiple joint action on the lat pull machine solicits all arm flexors both concentrically and eccentrically. With a straight back, pull the bar down behind the neck or in front of the chest. The head remains upright throughout and is not lowered into the neck. Ensure a controlled release of the weight.

9 Bench press

This exercise can be performed either on a machine or with a barbell. The upper body can lie either horizontally or diagonally on a suitable surface, with the hips and knees bent at 90 degrees. It is essential to work with a spotter when training with free weights and heavy weights.

10 Bench pull

The opposite action can also be performed lying prone and pulling the barbell up from the floor. The lower legs are bent at right angles in order to avoid curving the back.

11 Wrist curl

In a sitting position, rest the elbows on the thighs and raise and lower the barbell with the wrist action only.

12 Shoulder shrug with barbell

In a standing position, with slightly bent knees and a straight back, hold the barbell down in front with straight arms and move it by raising and lowering the shoulders.

13 Back machine

Slow stretching of the hanging back and slow, careful lowering of the back. Ensure correct movement execution; the back should not be raised above the horizontal.

14 Crunches

a. Crunches: The knees are bent at a 90-degree angle and held steady in the air, while the upper body starting from the head is slowly rolled up and then back down again.

b. Crossover crunch: In the same starting position, cross your hands behind your head and again roll slowly up, bringing your elbow toward the opposite knee, and repeat on the other side.

The previous exercises should be taught in a gym or weight room by an experienced weight training instructor or coach and combined with exercises from the sections, In the Gym or at Home and Functional Stretching. A strength training session is composed of a **warm-up**, **main section** (circuit) and a **cool-down**.

Circuit Training

In the main section, exercises can be chosen in the form of a circuit. The exercises chosen should activate as many appropriate muscles groups as possible, with the emphasis on those of the legs and hips. For the arms, go for multiple-joint pulling and pushing exercises (e.g., pulley machine, bench press), which each use several muscles. When sequencing the exercises, make sure that you allow a rest phase for the muscles used in each exercise by training a completely different muscle group. To avoid one-sided training, certain exercises should occasionally be replaced by others. Exercises like the leg press or squats with the barbell should always be part of the program, though. Exercises for back and abs should be slotted between them and should also be performed on a daily basis.

Circuit Program C_1:
Exercise sequence 1, 7, 13, 5, 9, 14, 4, 6, 2

Circuit Program C_2:
Exercise sequence 2, 8, 13, 7, 3, 14, 9, 6, 11, 4

For a more intensive strength endurance workout, do station training, in which all reps are done at one station before moving on to the next. This should train different muscle groups. In station training, the number of reps is roughly 20 per set, and 3–8 sets are performed. The rests last about two minutes. The disadvantage of station training is that it is very time consuming.

4.3.2   In the Gym or at Home

Strength training can also be done effectively in a gym or even at home—primarily with bodyweight exercises—which, when done correctly and in combination with strength training on the bike, can replace weight training on machines and free weights. For strength training in the gym or at home, there are two main methods: dynamic and static. It is important to exercise not only the leg muscles, but also the arms, abs, back and shoulders. At high performance level, train the whole body with emphasis on the legs; at grass-roots level, emphasize the core muscles when training.

Below are selected strengthening exercises to be done in the gym or at home, grouped according to body part.

What to Watch Out For
The number of reps and sets should be geared to age, fitness and goal; for example a keep-fit biker should use lower numbers of reps and sets while the trained performance biker should go for the higher numbers. If you train so hard that you suffer severe muscle soreness after every workout, you are definitely training too hard; avoid muscle soreness or extreme exhaustion. The numbers after the muscle groups again correspond to the individual muscles in the illustrations in chapter 2.

Leg Muscles
Calf muscle **39**, **44**
See strength training exercise **5**

Shin muscles **32**, **33**, **34**
Sitting on the floor, bend the outstretched legs at the ankle by raising the toes and gradually lowering them, keeping your heels on the floor. A partner can press down on the toes for a deeper stretch. Perform 2–4 sets of 10–20 reps.

Quads, calves, glutes **25**, **26**, **31**, **39**, **40**, **44**
There are a whole series of exercises for the quads.

  a. Squat down against a wall as if sitting on an imaginary stool and hold this position for 15–60 seconds, keeping your back straight and pressed against the wall and your arms hanging down by your sides (static exercise).
  b. Depending on fitness, perform 2–4 sets of 10–30 tuck jumps over a bench (i.e., back and forth).
  c. See strength training exercise 3

Core Muscles
Abs training **6**, **7**, **8**
See strength training exercise **14**

Back muscles **3**, **9**, **10**, **12**, **40**
Lie facedown on the floor with legs out behind you and arms in front. Raise the stretched feet a little from the floor. Now with the arms, perform slow, sweeping pull-ups. Bring the arms alternately fast forward and backward close past the body.

Push-ups 3, 4, 5, 6, 7, 8, 9, 10, 14, 15

The push-up is, when performed correctly, an excellent exercise for the back and abs and for the arms and shoulders. It is important to maintain good body tension and to keep the body straight. Different variations with narrow or wide arm positions and fast or slow movements are possible. The number of reps is totally dependent on the ability of the individual. Ideally, carry out three sets of a pre-determined number of reps.

Arms and Shoulders

Another option for the arm and shoulder muscles, along with the strengthening exercises, is medicine ball exercises, which are borrowed from back therapy training. It is beyond the scope of this book to go into back therapy training in detail.

Medicine ball training involves two athletes throwing a 3-6-kilogram medicine ball to each other in several sets, with different throwing and pushing techniques. A program for strengthening the core and arm muscles should be performed daily in order to prevent postural defects due to one-sided effort on the bike.

Jumps Circuit

Almost all kinds of jumps are suitable for strengthening the leg muscles, but hops should only be performed once a high strength level has been attained. In the gym, it is very easy to set up a jumps circuit consisting of four to ten exercises that can be done consecutively or individually. Jumping exercises also improve speed strength. Good exercise ideas for a jumps circuit can be found in the book Power Plyometrics also published by Meyer & Meyer Verlag.

An exercise that improves both strength and endurance is jumping rope, which is also great for training strength endurance. A program for the legs should always include several different exercises.

4.4   Strength Circuit

This small circuit has proved to be an ideal way of fitting in your daily strength training at home, as it requires little time and space to perform. The six selected exercises each load multiple joints and train all muscles groups relevant for mountain bikers.

This circuit can also be done quickly after the main workout and before the shower. Perform 2–5 sets with very short rests in between sets (a few minutes). Perform each exercise with no rest in between in the sequence below.

Exercise name	Reps	Muscle groups	Equipment
1. Push-up	15	Arms, chest, back	
2. Calf rise	30 each foot	Calf	Wall
3. Crunches	15	Abs	
4. Reverse push-up	15	Triceps	Bed
5. Prone lie pull-up	20	Back	
6. Squat jumps	20	Quads, glutes	

The number of reps should be adapted to individual fitness levels.

1. Perform a normal push-up (slow and fast).
2. Facing the wall, stand on one straightened leg, then extend the ankle (calf muscle) to raise your body.
3. With legs in the air, keep the hips, knees and ankles at 90 degree angles.
4. Perform reverse push-ups on the edge of the bed.
5. Lie pronated, looking at the floor with legs and feet extended 5-cm off the floor, and perform very slow pull-up movements with the arms.
6. Squat jumps is a kind of standing jump with completely fixed, erect upper body and fists clenched next to the head. When in the crouch position, knees are bent at roughly 90 degrees.

Train Year-Round

Year-round strength training is necessary for all mountain bikers, from keep-fit and grass-roots level right up to elite level, although the objective may vary. While at elite and competitive level, the aim is primarily specific performance improvement, strength training at grass-roots level instead is intended to prevent injury and protect the body from over-use and abnormal biomechanical stress. This aspect should, of course, still be addressed at elite level, as targeted training for postural and supporting muscles (i.e., core, shoulders, arms) is an effective way of preventing musculoskeletal injuries.

5

5 Functional Stretching

5.1 Why Stretch?

Many mountain bikers are constantly striving to improve their performance and think that the only way to do this is by training hard on the bike. However, training on the bike (on- or off-road) and strength training are only part of a complete and well-thought out training program.

As well as these active, strenuous training forms, all mountain bikers, from cross-country or downhill specialists to licensed or just keep-fit riders, should also include stretching in their training plan to aid relaxation and recovery. It takes only 10–15 minutes a day and results can be obtained quickly. The body will show its gratitude for this extra effort with fewer injuries and better performance in training and racing. Stretching is equally as important as functional strengthening as a preventive measure in mountain bike training.

5.2 What Does Stretching Achieve?

Stretching as an activity was popularized in the US in the 1960s by Bob Anderson; it would be an exaggeration to call it a sport. As many targeted muscles as possible are stretched according to certain movement patterns. It is preferable to work downward from the head to the feet.

A mountain biker's muscles are susceptible to shortening and cramping. This is due to the cyclical contractions involved in the pedaling action and the continuous, static loading of large muscles groups, which is exacerbated by the unnatural posture on the mountain bike or racing bike. Muscle shortening can cause incorrect biomechanical stress or non-physiologically sound compensatory movements, which in turn can overload other ligaments, tendons, muscles and bones. In these cases, stretching serves to restore the natural muscle tone (i.e., the normal muscle tension).

The most important functions of stretching are explained briefly below:
- Injury prevention
- Acceleration of recovery
- Performance improvement
- Improved physical awareness

The increased elasticity and improved blood circulation prepare muscles and tendons for activity and are therefore less likely to be injured. In addition, overuse injuries caused by the constant pulling on shortened muscle tendons, and their insertions points on the bones can be avoided and treated.

After exercise, stretching causes metabolic stimulation that accelerates recovery.

Performance improvement is achieved due to enhanced muscle coordination and a more economical action of the stretched muscles. During muscle activity, the antagonist muscle must be actively stretched. For the working muscle, this means that as well as the strength required for each movement, extra strength must be applied to stretch the corresponding antagonist, which is responsible for the countermovement. If this antagonist is shortened, the stretching work of the agonist is correspondingly greater. A practical example is the hamstring muscles, which must be stretched by the quadriceps every time the legs are extended. Regular stretching also eliminates knots in muscle, tendon and connective tissue, which again improves movement economy.

Finally, stretching improves physical awareness and physical perception. The smallest changes within the muscles are perceived more quickly and with greater intensity, and this heightened body awareness can be used to actively prevent injuries (by rest or training reduction) and manage training.

Stretching Techniques
The most important principle in stretching is to concentrate on the body part concerned during the stretch in order to be totally aware of the sensations of tension and relaxation. Breathing should be even, relaxed and never forced. Calm breathing and self-awareness make stretching perfect for relaxation and an important mental or psychological component of the pre- and post-race routine of many athletes.

Stretching should never hurt, although a light, pleasant pulling sensation is normal. There are several different stretching techniques, two of which are presented next.

Static Stretching

The static stretch is the easiest to learn and is the most important and best-known form of stretching. Static stretching is deliberately slow and steady. The movement is not externally discernible and involves no bouncing or bobbing. The stretching process should last between 10 and 30 seconds per exercise and per body side A pleasant tension should be felt in the muscles, which yields slightly toward the end of the stretch. At this point, the stretch can be intensified and held for another 10 to 30 seconds. The stretch time can be counted quietly to start with, but over time an improved sense of timing will make this unnecessary. If necessary, every exercise can be performed several times to increase the stretch.

The following exercises relate to the static method but may also be performed using the CHRS method.

CHRS (Contract–Hold–Relax–Stretch) Method

The CHRS method is a more complex method in which each exercise is divided into four parts. The targeted muscle is first contracted, then held, then relaxed and finally stretched. This sequence is carried out in the cycle two to four times per muscle or muscle group. The muscle can usually be stretched further after every relaxation. This method is more effective but also more strenuous and more time-consuming. Try out both methods under the guidance of an instructor and then choose one.

Stretching has nothing to do with suffering, pain and gritting your teeth. If the tension in the muscles is too great, reduce it slightly by changing the joint angles. Bouncing and jerking activate what is known as the stretch reflex and cause further cramping in the muscles. If a muscle is suddenly strongly stretched, for example, by bouncing or jerking, the muscle spindles are activated, leading to a sudden contraction of the muscle by the spinal cord. The stretch reflex protects a muscle from over-stretching or tearing.

Before the stretching program, you should warm up a little by running in place, hopping or riding on the roller without a brake (5 min). Wear comfortable clothing (jogging suit) and, if possible, sit on a comfortable surface in a warmish room. Stretching exercises can, however, be done anytime, anywhere (e.g., at work during breaks or while waiting).

One provision to keep in mind is that in the case of injuries or after operations on the musculoskeletal system, stretching should be avoided or only performed after taking medical advice.

The elite athlete should stretch daily, especially after training and, depending on the kind of training (gym or weight) also before and during. The keep-fit biker should also ideally stretch daily, but at least on training days.

5.3   Stretching Program

The figures behind the body parts relate to the muscles in figures 2.4–2.7.

1. Muscles of the front and back of the neck (*trapezius, sternocleidomastoid*, deep neck muscles) **1, 3, 13**
The head is bent to the front, left and right for 30 seconds each, thereby stretching the neck muscles. The shoulders should remain horizontal throughout. Stretch the head as far as possible to the left and hold the position, then repeat to the right.

2. Shoulder (*deltoid, serratus anterior, latissimus dorsi*) **5, 11, 14**

Circle the arms and shoulders to relax your shoulders. Stretch the shoulder girdle by bringing the elbows above the head and placing the palm of the hand between the shoulder blades. Hold this position for about 10–30 seconds per side. This significantly increases the flexibility of the shoulders.

3 Upper arms and shoulders

(*m. deltoideus, m. triceps brachii*) **14**, **15**

One hand is passed under the chin and laid against the opposite shoulder. Push the elbow toward the shoulder with the other hand.

4 Forearms and wrists

(Forearms and finger muscles) **22**, **23**

Gripping the handlebars causes the forearm muscles to cramp up. Overextend the wrists with straight, raised arms, with the palm of the hand facing away from the body and the fingertips pointing downward. The fingers can also be stretched separately in this way.

5 Core (*m. serrati, m. latissimus dorsi*) **5**, **11**

Stand with the feet roughly shoulder-width apart and bend the upper body to the side while at the same time bending one arm over the head and keeping the other resting on the thigh or pushing an imaginary object toward the floor.

6 Back and hamstrings

(*m. erector spinae*, hamstrings) **12**, **13**, **36**, **37**, **38**, **39**

Start by standing straight and raise your arms to make yourself very tall; then bring your arms down and start to slowly bend your head to your chest. First round your thoracic spine then your lumbar spine until finally your upper body is hanging down relaxed, and, keeping your legs straight, reach your hands down so they almost touch the feet. Then, equally slowly, straighten back up until you are tall again. In this exercise, like the others, make sure that you relax and tune out outside distractions when you perform it. This is easier to achieve with your eyes closed.

A fantastically relaxing exercise for the back is hanging. Hang from one or both arms from a bar or pole and hang for as long as you can hold the position.

7 Calf muscles (*m. gastrocnemius, m. soleus*) **39**, **44**

In the lunge position, support yourself with your hands against a wall or other stable object. The feet are parallel and facing forward, and the rear leg is straight. The front leg is bent until a stretch can be felt in the calf. The rear heel must remain on the floor. A stronger stretch of the Achilles tendon and the soleus can be achieved by bending the rear leg, but still keep that heel on the floor. The upper body is slightly more upright.

8 Hamstrings and calves (*ischiocrural muscles, m. gastrocnemius, m. soleus*) **36**, **37**, **38**, **39**

a. In the lunge position (feet pointing forward), bend forward keeping your back straight and your toes pulled back, so that you feel a stretch in your calf and hamstrings.

b. With the feet crossed, bend forward keeping your legs straight. Then swap the position of the feet.

9 Quadriceps (*m. quadriceps*) **25**, **26**, **31**

To aid balance, you can rest against a wall when stretching the quadriceps. Raise your left foot to the buttocks and grip the instep of the foot with the left hand. Pull it slowly toward the glutes until you can feel tension in the quads. The hips should be brought slightly forward, making sure that the thighs remain parallel to each other and the upper body is erect. Hold for 20–30 seconds per side.

10 Adductors (*m. adductor magnus, m. adductor longus*) **29, 35**

Stand in a wide side lunge position, with the feet parallel and facing forward. Bend one knee until the stretch can be felt on the inside of the thigh above the knee. This stretch position can also be performed in a forward lunge, but this stretches the back of the thighs (hamstrings) instead.

11 Quadriceps and shin muscles (*m. quadriceps, m. tibialis anterior, m. extensor digitorum longus, m. peronaeus longus*) **25, 26, 31, 32, 33**

Kneel down with the backs of your thighs and feet on the floor. After about 15 seconds, lift a knee with one hand, thus stretching the muscles in front of the shin.

12 Glutes (*gluteal muscles*) **40**

   a. Lie down on your back and stretch out your body. Then raise one leg and place the ankle of the other leg on the knee of the raised leg. Now link hands behind the raised thigh and pull it slightly toward you, keeping your hips on the floor. If the stretch is not strong enough, push the knee outward slightly.

   b. In a sitting position, place the sole of the left foot on the right knee. Both legs are bent, and the upper body now leans forward on to the left leg. You can support yourself on your elbows. The stretch is mainly felt in the left buttock and in the top of the left hamstring. After about 40 seconds, change sides.

These exercises constitute a basic program that can be supplemented by other exercises. The previous exercises can be performed both before and after racing and also for recovery purposes at home in the evenings.

5.4   Stretching on the Mountain Bike

It is possible to give tired muscles a stretch even on your bike. A few exercises are described next. They should only be done on flat terrain and not at high speeds, for example after a strenuous climb or a body-tensing downhill. Most exercises on the bike are modifications of the exercises presented before. Exercises 7, 8 and 9 can also be performed during a race and are mainly intended to prevent cramping. As soon as the first signs of cramping are felt, perform the appropriate exercise several times during the ride, if possible.

**Following is an exercise program for
while riding the mountain bike or racing bike.**

1 Neck
(*m. trapezius, m. sternocleidomastoideus*, deep neck muscles) 1, 3, 13
Hyperextending the cervical spine when cycling often causes muscular cramps, which can be very painful.

Bend your head to the left and right for 5 seconds in each direction. This can be intensified by pulling with one arm. Likewise, with a rounded back, place your chin on your chest, supporting the stretch a little with one arm (but be careful!). See illustration for exercise 1.

2 Spine and core (*m. trapezius, m. latissimus dorsi, m. erector spinae*, small neck muscle) 3, 11, 12, 13
While riding with no hands, stretch out and stretch your arms up to make yourself as tall as possible.

3 Shoulder girdle (*m. trapezius, m. deltoideus, m. subscapularis, m. infraspinatus, m. teres major and minor*) 3, 9, 10, 14, 18
Grip the handlebars and straighten your arms to raise both shoulders to your ears (5 sec), and then push them down. Next, take one hand off the handlebar, let your arm hang down loosely and circle the whole arm a few times forward and backward.

4 Forearm muscles (forearm and finger muscles) 22, 23
Starting position: Ride free-handed.
Stretch the forearm muscles fatigued and cramped by the static work, braking and gear changing. Stretch one arm with the palm of the hand upward and outward and with the other hand pull the fingers down. Hold the exercise for 20 seconds. See illustration for exercise 4.

5 Hands and arms (forearm and finger muscles) **22, 23**
With one hand on the handlebar, the other, with the back of the hand and the fingers on top, put your hand on your hip for 10 seconds until you can feel a stretch in the hand, forearm and shoulder. This relaxes hands that are tired from gripping the handlebar. Wrist circling increases the relaxation.

6 Back (*m. trapezius, m. latissimus dorsi, m. erector spinae*, small neck muscles) **3, 11, 12, 13**
The back can often feel tense and sore, which can be alleviated by vigorous stretching.
    a. Holding the handlebar normally, first round then arch your back. Repeat both movements several times.
    b. While the left hand holds the handlebar, bring your right arm under your left arm so that the upper body twists as you stretch the core muscles (5–10 sec per side).

7 Hamstrings (*ischiocrural muscles, m. gastrocnemius, m. soleus*) **36, 37, 38, 39**
The hamstrings can be stretched quite successfully on the bike. Lift yourself out of the saddle and bring the left pedal forward to the 9 o'clock position. With the balls of the feet resting on the pedals, lower your heels, straighten your legs and lower your erect upper body forward (5–10 sec). Then repeat on the other leg.

8 Quadriceps (*m. quadriceps, m. tibialis anterior, m. extensor digitorum longus, m. peronaeus longus*) **25, 26, 31, 32, 33**
The quads can also be stretched while cycling, although it does require a little riding expertise and good balance. Lift one foot off the pedal and grip the ankle with the hand on the same side. Now pull the knee back slightly until you feel a stretch.

9 Calves and Achilles tendon (*m. gastrocnemius, m. soleus*) **38, 39, 45**
Raise yourself out of the saddle, keeping the crank vertical, and push the lower leg down. Push the heel of that leg down until you can feel a stretch. In order to transfer the stretch to the Achilles tendon, bend the knee of the straightened leg slightly. The last three exercises (7, 8 and 9) are suitable for eliminating annoying cramps, particularly calf cramps.

Stretching and Running

Compared to cycling on the road and off-road, running is a very high-impact sport for the musculoskeletal system, as there is no bike to support your bodyweight. The result of the high mechanical, eccentric stress on the muscles caused by run-

ning is severe muscle shortening, which must be counteracted by stretching. The legs muscles in particular must be kept supple by using the previous exercises. Running training should always be followed by a stretching program.

Stretching and Strength Ttraining
Strength training is also highly stressful for the body, even though the eccentric component only features in certain types of exercise. In order to avoid injuries, warm-up should be followed by an intensive stretching program. The muscles used may also be stretched between exercises. After the workout, cool down with stretching exercises. A few new studies claim that stretching during strength training reduces the effectiveness of the training. This should be ignored though, as the main priority is the prevention of injury.

6

6 Training Management

6.1 Be Your Own Coach

"Be your own coach" is an American phrase, which is typical of the American approach to sport, particularly endurance sport. You are in the best position to know your body, feel the exhaustion, the strength and are also best placed to decide what is right for you in terms of training. However, a certain amount of knowledge is still required for this, which this book and others like it attempt to provide. It goes without saying that if you are lucky enough to have a good coach, you should be pleased and certainly not trying to get rid of him! Two heads are better than one, and by actively participating in the training planning and structuring with your coach you will achieve more, and the collaboration will be more successful. Absolute novices would find it hard alone and should seek the collaboration of experienced mountain bikers or coaches and then gradually work out their own idea of a structured training plan.

A sensible, self-constructed training plan based on a few important training rules guarantees good performance development. It is up to you to determine a sensible proportion of flexibility and highly structured training in order to be successful while also having fun. Solemnly and unthinkingly sticking 100% to a rigid program cannot achieve this. Listen to your body and decide what works for you and what doesn't. If you don't feel good after training or racing, rest for a day.

6.2 Your Own Training Plan

Now for a description of the procedure involved in drawing up a training plan according to the important principles of time management. First, the division of the phases should be examined in more detail. If you are preparing a training plan for the first time, you should allow yourself time to do it and, above all, obtain the advice of experienced mountain bikers in order to avoid possible mistakes. Often, novices and, in particular, ambitious athletes tend to overestimate their time budget, their motivation and their ability to recuperate. They make plans they cannot stick to, which may result in a completely incorrect build-up, low performance level and possibly a state of overtraining.

The opinion that only one training plan or one method can lead to elite level performance is fortunately mistaken. Different training methods lead to the goal,

for everyone reacts differently to the training content, hence the importance of experimenting with different methods. What works for one cyclist does not necessarily work for another.

Reaching peak performance not only involves planning and executing training but also adjusting it. So while there are many different ways of preparing for success, amendments to the training plan are required in almost every case. Performance is consolidated and optimized with respect to the season's goal through systematic periodization and cyclization of intensity and volume.

If a training error is identified and rectified immediately, nothing is lost, but if training errors or poor performance are ignored, it is usually impossible to reach the goal you have set for the season.

Analysis of the Previous Year
Training planning also involves an analysis of the previous year. Many training errors can be identified using the notes in your training diary. These errors must definitely be addressed when preparing the new training plan and should be kept in mind in the following season, especially in the case of poor form. Tips for analyzing the previous year can be found in chapter 6.4.

Planning From Year to Year
When preparing your training plan, you need to take into account not just the preceding and coming years but also your long-term development. A continuous improvement in performance due to moderate increases in training is much better and also leads to less frequent drops in form and injuries than excessive increases in the annual training volume. Unstable performances can often be observed in the case of young amateurs, who do not yet have a solid foundation of endurance training. The annual training volume is measured in hours, of which a high proportion (about 60%) should be **BE 1** training.

The principle of continuous workload increase involves increases of, at most, approximately 15% at elite level. Higher loading increases of over 20% to about 40% are only possible in mountain biking at regional level. Only beginners are allowed to double their total training volume the following year, if appropriate. The higher the performance level, the more gradual the planned loading increases. Rehab bikers and beginners should be cautious, though, for physical exercise must be approached very gradually in order to avoid possible health risks.

Top cyclists who decide to stop competing at elite level should never reduce their training by more than 50% from one year to the next in order to eliminate any health risks. In the former GDR, endurance athletes at the end of the career were given training plans that reduced their training workload gradually. A basic training workload of about 200–250 hours per year should, however, be maintained in any case.

This is how it's done:

First step: Performance testing and current state analysis

Once the athlete is familiar with the training and racing demands of mountain biking, the next step is to establish his current state of physical fitness. Without this it is very hard to know what kind of training to prescribe. Only once the fitness state is determined can it be assessed whether the envisaged volumes and intensities are at the correct level. A fitness test does not necessarily mean a laboratory-based performance test. A time-trial result, the outcome of your last race or, even simpler, an experienced mountain biker's physical awareness, are enough to give you or other people an idea of your form. If this assessment is incorrect and the training based upon it turns out to be over or under challenging, the plan must be adjusted.

The performance diagnosis should also be accompanied by an analysis of the athlete's general circumstances (i.e., social environment, job).

In addition, previous years of training workload and form development should also be examined as part of the fitness assessment. Excessive annual workload increases in terms of total volume usually have a negative effect on the form development. A race and training analysis of the previous year is the final stage in the evaluation process.

Second step: Realistic goal-setting

The setting of goals for the new training year is a critical part of the planning process, and they should be

written down. As well as setting race goals (e.g., finishing position in the regional championships), specific goals, such as improving downhill technique or improving strength endurance, must be set, which may even include more detailed goals such as focusing on certain cycling techniques. A goal for keep-fit bikers could be mastering a climb or reaching the top of a pass in a certain time.

All training goals must be realistic, as over-ambitious goals are soon forgotten, while unchallenging goals are not sufficiently inspiring.

Ideally, goals should be discussed with training partners, a coach or other experienced bikers. If you are very keen, you can formulate detailed goals for all core mountain biking skills that, during the course of the training year, can be checked off when they are achieved. You should always allow for the possibility of modifying your goals slightly during the course of the season.

Third step: Race planning
The third step consists of obtaining and checking out the race calendar (and if possible also for road races). The keep-fit or bike tour rider finds the dates for bike tours or marathons, while the racing biker uses the racing calendar to plan his racing season. Two or three seasonal peaks can be aimed for, but one should take priority. It is a good idea to set seasonal highpoints for a date in the late summer. It is not easy to peak early in the season (i.e., for certain qualifying races), and the preparation phases require great commitment.

Fourth step: Division into phases
The first planning step is dividing the training phases (preparation phases, racing phase, transition phase) and subdividing them into shorter training sections: cycles or stages (4–6 wks). Usually phases are divided as described in chapter 3, although deviations from this standard scheme, which aims for a peak in the summer, are possible. This periodization is shown in graphic form in chapter 3. The content and goal-setting for each phase are also formulated, and the possibility of training camps is also considered.

Once the phases are organized with start and end dates, the number of microcycles in each phase is calculated. A microcycle corresponds to one week.

Within the phases, the cycles are now highlighted, which comprisetwo to five microcycles with increasing workload followed by a recovery microcycle.

All the weeks of the training year are now planned, and each phase and every four- to six-week cycle have been filled with specific training content. Even the races have now been added as accurately as possible. The detailed planning of each individual training session is done immediately before the start of each phase.

A large A3 sketch pad is perfect for planning the year. It is important that all comments are written down.

Fifth step: Detailed planning of the four- to six-week cycles
The final step involves planning individual training sessions for the upcoming four- to six-week cycle, using the simple method of block building. The pattern is: increasing workload two to four days followed by a rest day, then two to four weeks of increasing workload followed by a recovery week.

The training sessions all feature the following factors:
- Training goal (e.g., improving anaerobic mobilization)
- Training method (e.g., endurance method with indications of gear ratio and cadence)
- Volume (e.g., duration or distance)
- Intensity (e.g., BE 1)

Check Training Plan Using Performance Tests
As described in the next section, performance and also the training plan must be tested at regular intervals. The dates for these tests must be included in the training plan when it is drawn up, and they can take the form of performance tests or time-trials. These tests take place at the beginning or the end of the phase and should be undertaken in a rested state. A fitness test should be carried out at the start of every preparation phase.

6.3   Training Plan Modifications

Training should be part of a feedback control system. Training results must be tested at regular intervals and the results used to manage the whole process. Race results should also be included to evaluate performance, but the many possible factors affecting the race result must be taken into account.

Pay attention to physical signs.
A quite critical factor in the evaluation of individual form is how your body feels, which is usually very accurate. Many mountain bikers and other athletes have problems with this, though, and find it hard to evaluate sensations in the muscles and the rest of the body during exercise.

Only after several years of mountain biking experience do you develop an awareness of your body's little signs, which can often be more informative than performance test results.

For example, experienced riders can tell by the amount of power in their legs when climbing stairs whether their muscles are in a recovered, performance-ready state. Or over the years they may have noticed that certain muscle aches and pains (e.g., twitching or itching) very often coincide with a period of peak form. The same is true for other physical signs such as fatigue, alertness, hunger, sleep, desire to train and willingness to train hard. Even the monitoring and recording of the resting and exercise heart rate, bodyweight and physical awareness during exercise help experienced athletes to evaluate their performance and modify their training accordingly.

However, there are also many cyclists who are completely incapable of interpreting their physical sensations and who even ignore their body's signals. This makes training management extremely difficult, as these athletes usually always train hard and often even mentally need this high training workload. In most cases, such athletes can only be convinced by scientific facts (i.e., diagnostic results), which are both time-consuming and expensive to perform, and the cost is in many cases not justified by the performance level of the athletes concerned.

Training Planning

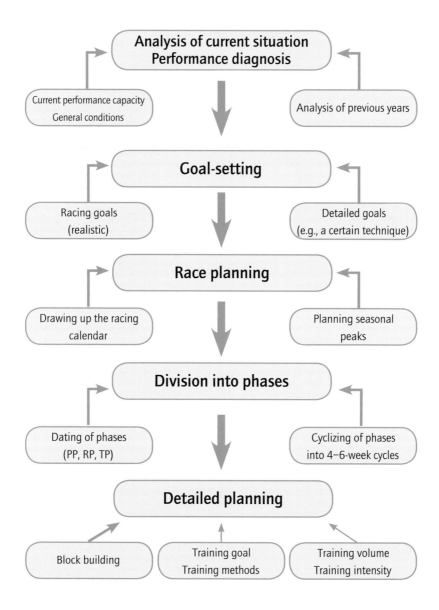

Fig. 6.1: Training planning in five steps

If your performance does plateau or even decline, you must ask yourself why this has happened. In most cases, the problem can be solved by modifying your training or taking a break from racing. Often the key factor is identified but not changed, possibly due to not wanting to deviate from a meticulously planned training program and still hoping for a delayed training effect. The change must be made, however.

Emergency Brake: Changing the Training Plan

Changing the training plan is a normal process and is an everyday part of high performance sport, as a training year rarely runs according to plan. However, the more experience one has, the better the planning and the less need for corrections. Basically, in the yearly plan only the phases and their contents are programmed. The detailed planning is best done a month to six weeks in advance. Changes within the individual microcycles are very common. However, if a change in the overall plan is required, something has gone wrong. Only by being open to change and reacting flexibly to changing conditions will you achieve success.

Following is a practical example with suggested solutions for such a case:

A cross-country biker was unable to train sufficiently during the preparation phase and started his racing season at the end of April, as always. Lack of conditioning in all zones, especially in the aerobic energy supply zone, meant that his race results left something to be desired. In races, he had no sense of his performance capacity. Training mainly involved doing really intensive training in each phase. This was made worse by the fact that the cyclist often trained with and tried to keep up with teammates who were in much better physical shape than him. The result of this overtraining was a stagnation in performance development and, on the mental level, a motivation crisis. Athletes in this situation often make the mistake of training even harder and then completely hitting rock bottom.

After about three or four races, every cyclist must be able to diagnose his poor form himself and trace it back to training errors. After one or two races, this is usually not yet possible, as the races at first usually cause great physiological adaptations and then maybe the cause was just an off-day. However, if you have noticed a serious problem with your form, a change in training strategy is unavoidable.

Rehabilitation Training

First, race participation should be postponed for at least two, better still, three, to four weeks, in order to be able to concentrate on training and in order to eliminate high racing loads in the threshold zone.

The reason for the poor performance is, in many cases, a very low level of basic endurance, which is the key conditioning foundation for a high racing tempo.

Day	1	2	3	4	5	6	7	8	9	10	11
Volume	–	–	–	+	++	–	+	++	+++	–	+
Intensity	CT	CT	CT	BE 1	BE 1	CT	BE 1	BE 1	BE 1	CT	BE 1
SE	–	–	–	–	–	–	–	–	–	–	+

Day	12	13	14	15	16	17	18	19	20	21
Volume	++	+++	–	++	+++	++++	–	++	+++	+++
Intensity	BE 1	BE 1		BE 1	BE 1	CT		BE 1	BE 1	BE 1
SE	++	–		+	++	–			Test	Test

Fig. 6.2: Example of rehabilitation training plan (+ = low, ++ = medium, +++ = high, ++++ = very high)

Anaerobic mobilization, essential in races for attacks, climbs and changes of tempo, also requires a good basic endurance foundation. As well as the poor aerobic energy supply, strength endurance is also inadequate. However, this puts the cyclist in a catch-22 situation, as the best way of developing strength endurance is by racing, which he is no longer allowed to do. The goal for the next training phase must be the improvement of basic endurance. If the cyclist is generally otherwise in good physical shape, strength endurance should also be developed in parallel. It is advisable to support this with functional general strength training (especially the core muscles) to raise general fitness levels and improve movement economy.

The new training phase, which can be called the build-up or rehabilitation phase, starts with a few days of physical rest, then stretching and other regenerative measures and, at most, light compensation training take place.

The diet should be very well-balanced during the build-up phase and should be highly nutritious, for overtraining can lead to deficiencies in certain nutrients. In addition, a new start in training offers the possibility for a fresh mental approach, equipped with new motivation and the feeling that now you are doing things right. This new attitude has a thoroughly positive effect on supporting factors such as diet, stretching and lifestyle. Another important factor is time. To make sure you do not go back to training too much or too intensively, it is vital to allow yourself time. If a training session must be dropped for an important reason, this is fine and the workout need not be caught up the following day.

After the recovery days, start with a two-day block of BE 1 training on the flattest possible terrain.

Then another recovery day, followed by several increasingly harder three-day blocks in the BE 1 zone, increasing the training volume slightly every day. The number of three-day blocks depends on the length of the phase. It is important to incorporate recovery days between the blocks, when your bike stays in the garage. After the second or third block, you can start to carry out strength endurance training on the bike, ideally on the first two days of the blocks. Loading should be increased slowly and cautiously. If necessary, the blocks may also be structured in reverse order (i.e., training gets easier).

Toward the end of the winter build-up phase, test your form (e.g., up a mountain or on a flat course over several minutes), riding almost flat-out and paying attention to how your body feels. How your legs feel and your heart rate give a particularly good indication of your form. The heart rate should react quickly, and normal exercise values should quickly be reached under such high loading. A rapid drop in heart rate post-exercise is also desirable (see chapter 3.3). A heart rate that increases too much or too little is an indication of a budding infection or a recovery deficit.

This rehabilitation training phase should normally not fail to have the desired effect. The previous training diagram deliberately avoids giving training volumes so that it is not limited to only one performance category. The volumes in this phase move from build-up to the highest for those recommended for each category.

Comments

To be successful, you need to experiment with new methods, for many roads lead to Rome and peak performance, as long as they respect defined rules of training methodology. Only by trying out new training methods and sensing their effects on your own body can you assess whether or not they work for you. It is advisable to try this kind of experimentation toward the end of the season, in any case, after your main races are over. For example, try training at maximum intensity or with a very high proportion of strength training, and observe the reaction of your body. By varying and changing the emphasis of your training and racing (i.e., choice of races), you may even see a jump in form that will enable you to break through performance barriers.

You can also experiment with changes in your diet.

6.4   Training Diary

It is advisable to keep a training diary in which to accurately document training and racing data.

The Training Planner

The most important part of a training diary is the actual calendar in which all information relevant for training and racing are noted. As well as data relating just to the training session, such as duration, distance, location and content of the workout, information on the rider's physiological state must also be documented. This includes measurements taken daily, such as resting heart rate, weight, how you feel (scale of 1–10) and comments on your health, such as amount and quality of sleep. The weather and other supplementary information should also be noted. In another block, you can also note whether stretching or an exercise program were carried out.

This amount of data that needs to be recorded may at first appear off-putting, but the effort is worth it for the ambitious cyclist. Ultimately, everyone must decide for themselves how many of the empty fields he completes daily and which he completes only occasionally or never. In the recording of training parameters, there are no limits to the detail you can go into, as countless other factors may be recorded. The aforementioned parameters do, however, represent a meaningful selection.

The last part of the training diary is used for the evaluation and analysis of the recorded training and racing data. This part does require a little work, if it is not continuously updated and only worked on at the end of the season. Special forms are filled in with the respective weekly averages of the different parameters and the data points collated in a graph. Certain events or race results are highlighted by arrows with visible comments. This graphic display of the training parameters very often allows connections to be spotted that otherwise would remain hidden. If you are unsure about a section, you can always look in the preceding part of the calendar to analyze connections in detail.

After the analysis, training is more detailed and productive when done in a group with a coach or experienced cyclists than when done alone, the main points or main conclusions should be noted and definitely incorporated into the training plan of the following season.

This process of data collection over several years enables a really targeted training planning and management, ultimately paving the way for peak performance.

Investing in a Training Diary
Filling in a training diary takes fewer than five minutes a day, a minimal amount of time with a great benefit. If you don't want to pay for a training diary, you can make your own out of photocopied pages in a folder.

The Importance of Regularity
It is essential to make regular diary entries. It is possible to assess a cyclist's training motivation by the way the training diary is kept. Usually, accurate and uninterrupted entries indicate a conscientious approach to training.

Evaluation and Analysis
By regularly entering data in the diary and evaluating it, errors and deficiencies can be spotted and rectified during the same training year.

The first step of training analysis is the comparison of the actual training performed with that which was planned. Are there significant discrepancies?

In another step, on a weekly or monthly basis, the resting heart rate and weight values together with the daily sense of physical well-being are linked to the size of the workload. Displayed in graphic form, overloading can now quite clearly be identified due to incorrect training volume.

If the periods when the cyclist felt good and the races in which he performed well are now highlighted in color, it is easy to see which type of training and which loading volume lead to good performances. Also loading structures that have exactly the opposite effect can be spotted immediately. Days of illness are highlighted in color in the table and in the calendar section.

Fig. 6.3: Training diary

	Mon AM	Mon PM	Tues AM	Tues PM	Wed AM	Wed PM	Thurs AM	Thurs PM	Fri AM	Fri PM	Sat AM	Sat PM	Sun AM	Sun PM	TOTAL
Type of training (mins) — Basic endurance 1 (BE 1)	55.00	75.00	55.00	90.00	55.00	55.00	55.00	135.00		60.00	135.00			240.00	1010
Training content — TOTAL	55	75	55	90	55	55	55	135		60	135			240	1010
Training — Daily distance (km)	22.0	32.0	22.0	38.0	22.0	22.0	22.0	56.0		25.0	58.0			100.0	419.0
Training — Average km/h	24.00	25.60	24.00	25.33	24.00	24.00	24.00	24.89		25.00	25.78			25.00	24.7
Training — Heart rate in BE 1 zone	118	119	119	128	126	121	128	126		114	127			127	123.0
General — Recovery		20.0				20.0		20.0		20.0	20.0			20.0	120.0
General — Strength training															
General — Alternative exercise															
Biorhythms — Sleep duration		8.00	8.00		8.50		8.00		9.00		8.00			8.50	8.3
Biorhythms — Resting heart rate		57	53		61		58		56		49			54	55.4
Biorhythms — Bodyweight		85.0	84.6		82.7		82.8		82.6		82.6			82.9	83.3
Racing — Racing time															
Racing — Daily distance covered															

Training zones: S4, S3, SS, ST, PZ, DZ, BE 2, BE 1, CT

Type of training / Training content / Training zones row labels:
Compensation (CT), Basic endurance 1, Frequency-oriented (SP), Strength-oriented (ST), Peak zone, Speed training, Speed-strength (# reps), Strength endurance, Intensive strength endurance

Training Affects Different People in Different Ways

As training is a very individual process and the same workout can affect two athletes very differently, results of this kind are very valuable for training planning. For this reason, all specific training tips must be relativized and tried out first; although certain basic principles, as stated in this book, do apply to everyone.

A detailed description of the possible configurations of all parameters would be excessive at this point. A training diary is especially helpful for those mountain bikers who do not have access to an experience coach. Over the years, errors can be eliminated and training optimized.

Training Diary on the Computer

For some time now, various training diary programs for the computer have been on the market, which, although they do a lot of the work for you (calculations and graphs), are really inflexible. A great disadvantage is the need to possess a notebook that requires daily feeding with the most up-to-date information. But when it becomes too difficult to have a "database" with them in training camps or at races, in order to work on the training diary, a traditional paper training diary, like the training planner in pocket book format, is ideal.

Ideal for the cyclist:

7

7 Nutrition

7.1 Fundamentals of Mountain-Bike-Specific Nutrition

In recent years, training volumes and intensities in elite endurance sports have increased to previously unimagined levels, and athletes have to consume large amounts of food (compared to the sedentary individual) in order to cope with these demands. Elite athletes should therefore be extremely careful that the food they eat is as high-quality and unadulterated as possible. Below, we start by looking at a few nutritional and physiological principles which form the basis of an adequate diet for the sport of mountain-biking.

Main function of food intake:
- Energy supply (for physical activity and vital functions)
- Build-up and maintenance of the body (cells, tissue)
- Regulation of the metabolic processes and health protection (in order to reduce the negative effects of the environment and high-performance sport on the body as much as possible)

There are four main food groups:

1. **Energy providers (fuel)**
   Carbohydrates (starches, sugars), fats, proteins

2. **Building materials**
   Water, protein (muscles, tendons, ligaments, cartilage), minerals and fats

3. **Regulatory and protective nutrients**
   Vitamins and trace elements (minerals)

4. **Functional food content**
   Fiber, food aroma, flavoring and coloring

Carbohydrates
Carbohydrates play a key role in sports nutrition. They ensure energy supply during high workloads, are easy to digest and in most cases also healthy. They have

two main advantages: They are both an oxygen-efficient (per liter of oxygen consumed, they provide over 10% more energy than fats) and fast source of energy. In our food, two-thirds of the energy supplied by carbohydrates should be in the form of complex carbohydrates (polysaccharides), starches and dextrin. Polysaccharides are multiple sugars (i.e., their molecules consist of several simple sugars), and starches (e.g., pasta, potatoes, rice) are the preferred form.

No more than a third of the overall carbohydrates should be composed of simple carbohydrates: mono- and disaccharides, which include the disaccharides sucrose (household sugar), lactose (milk sugar) and maltose (malt sugar) and the monosaccharides, which include glucose (dextrose), fructose (fruit sugar) and galactose.

For endurance athletes, carbohydrate intake should form at least 60% of the overall calorie amount.

Dietary fiber plays an important role for a high-carbohydrate diet, for a balanced blood sugar concentration during the course of the day, and for the digestion and a feeling of satiety after eating a meal.

Fats

While the amount of fats in the total energy amount should constitute about 25–30%, most Americans eat much more than this. Excessive fat consumption leads to the laying down of fatty deposits, increasing the risk for arterial sclerosis. Of the fats consumed by humans, 95% belong to the group of triglycerides and are used for energy production; about 5% of the fats are phospholipids and cholesterol, which are used as building materials. The triglycerides are split into glycerin and free fatty acids, absorbed in the small intestine by specialized cells and distributed into the circulation through the lymph system. What is not immediately burned for energy production is recomposed into triglycerides and stored. If the glycogen reserves are depleted during exercise, the stored fat deposits are remobilized and recruited for energy production. The fats can, however, only burn when carbohydrates are burned; if the carbohydrates are highly depleted, fat-burning is also diminished, leading to a drop in performance capacity.

Fatty foods prolong the length of time food spends in the stomach and, therefore, delay the absorption of food. They slow down the replenishment of the glycogen reserves that is so important for recovery after exercise.

Proteins

The proportion of protein should be roughly between 10 and 15% of the total energy requirement. The importance of proteins for performance in endurance sports was underestimated for a long time. The daily steak as the basic prerequisite of a sports-appropriate and performance-boosting diet is now passé.

Proteins are mainly used in the cells as building and transporting substances and only in small amounts for energy production.

Proteins consist of chains of different amino acids. There are 20 different known amino acids, of which humans must consume 10 in their diet; we are able to synthesize the rest ourselves. In the stomach and small intestine, the proteins are split by enzymes and absorbed as amino acids into the blood. If the specific amino acid requirement in a cell is met, the amino acids are converted into fat and glycogen and also used for energy production.

Cape Eric:
The riders at the back
must eat dust!

For the endurance athlete, the recommended protein requirement is 1.2–1.5 grams per kilogram bodyweight. An additional protein intake, in the form of powders for example, is not necessary. If more protein is consumed, this in no way means that more muscle mass will be built. Instead, the surplus amount is burnt up as third-choice fuel and eliminated again as urine, which puts too much stress on the kidneys. You must drink a lot to prevent dehydration in the case of high protein consumption. The other part of the excess protein calories is stored as fat.

Water

Almost all metabolic processes require water as an essential medium. In endurance sports such as mountain biking, the body loses a lot of water when breathing air and sweating, and this loss of water (dehydration) means that the metabolic processes can no longer take place at the required pace. The metabolism slows down, leading to a drop in performance.

In intensive physical activity, the body can lose between one and two liters of water per hour of activity. During a training ride, the water loss is around half to one liter per hour; in a ride lasting several house (e.g., 5-hr workout), the water loss is two and a half to five liters.

Of all food deficiencies, the lack of water has the most rapid and serious effect on performance. A rise in body temperature can be a result of the increased sweat production in the case of a water deficiency. For this reason, make sure you drink plenty of water before a workout.

Lost water can be replaced, as was usual until quite recently in cycling, either with pure water, by mixing your own drink or buying one of the expensive sports drinks promoted by advertising. The advantage of sports drinks is that as well as the necessary water, they also provide carbohydrates, minerals and vitamins that are also lost in sweat.

The concentration of these drinks is a problem for the manufacturers; on the one hand, they have to be in a form that can be drunk quickly, and on the other they should still contain enough carbohydrate to counteract any decline in performance. For most mountain bikers, a concentration of 5–8 % carbohydrate is suitable. So, 5–8 grams of carbohydrate is stirred into 100 milliliters of water (25–40 g in a 500 ml drinking bottle). Higher concentrations (more than 10%) can cause indigestion and stomach problems. Because fruit juice usually has a sugar concentration in excess of 10%, it can be diluted with a good, slightly carbonated magnesium, calcium and potassium-rich mineral water in the ratio 1:1. The good old apple juice spritzer is an excellent, tasty and also still very cheap sports drink.

Which drinks can the athlete drink on a daily basis?
- Mineral water (a lot of magnesium, calcium, potassium and relatively little sodium)
- Fruit juices (especially freshly squeezed)
- Fruit juice spritzers
- Milk, milk shakes (1.5% fat)
- Tea
- Malt beer
- Vegetable juice (ideally without added sugar)

After exercise, carbohydrate and mineral-rich fruit juice spritzers or even cola in quantities to refill the glycogen reserves are particularly recommended.

How do you drink during exercise?
- Slowly, in small sips.
- 150 milliliters roughly every 15 minutes, not the whole bottle at once.
- Never exercise if you are low on fluids or feel thirsty.

In training and racing, it is a good idea to drink regularly and before you start to feel thirsty. At this point, you have already lost too much fluid. If the weather is very hot, you can take a bottle of frozen water and drink the melting, cool water. Conversely, in cold weather you can take a thermos flask of tea.

Vitamins
Vitamins are organically essential nutrients that influence the metabolism in multiple places despite only being present in extremely small concentrations. They are not used for fuel by the body and provide no energy. The importance of vitamins for increasing sporting performance capacity is often overestimated. If you are diagnosed with a vitamin deficiency though, supplements are necessary.

Minerals

Minerals are inorganic elements and compounds, which are very important for the human body as building and regulatory substances. They also include the trace elements, such as iron, zinc, chromium, selenium, copper, iodine, molybdenum, cobalt and manganese.

7.2   Nutrition for the Different Training Phases

Basic Nutrition

Nutrition for endurance sports (mountain biking) should be
- varied,
- low in fat,
- high in carbohydrate (ideally complex carbs) and
- contain high-quality protein.

How do you eat a high-carbohydrate diet?

Pasta, rice (both mainly as whole grain products), whole grain products (whole grain bread, biscuits, all kinds of muesli), potatoes, legumes (beans, peas), vegetables and fruit as well as fruit juices are excellent sources of carbohydrates, which—compared to refined products—also contain a lot of other valuable nutrients. White sugar or white flour, for example, contain only empty calories, as they contain no other nutrients such as vitamins, fiber or minerals in addition to the sugar or starch molecules. Make sure food is as natural and unprocessed as possible and avoid ready meals and products, which almost always contain additives (e.g., flavor enhancers, coloring, preservatives, emulsifying agents).

Why should I try to eat a low-fat diet?

Firstly, your consumption of visible fats (e.g., oil, butter, margarine and meat fat) must be deliberately reduced, and secondly, you need to be able to identify and avoid hidden fats. Hidden fats are mainly found in fatty sausage, fatty cheese, eggs, candy, sauces and fried foods. The aim of a low-fat diet is not the banning of all fat consumption, but rather the conscious selection of food, including the avoidance of unhealthy and fatty food. It is very important to differentiate between saturated and unsaturated, high-quality fatty acids, which, like linoleic acid, can reduce cholesterol levels unlike the saturated fatty acids. Fats that are liquid (i.e., dripping) at room temperature are of higher quality than solid ones.

Which foods contain high-quality protein combined with little fat?
Ideal protein sources are fat-free or low-fat dairy products, whole grain products, rice and pasta as well as almost all types of fish, poultry and low-fat cuts of beef, pork and lamb. But also legumes and cereal products are very low-fat sources of protein. By increasing consumption of vegetable protein, you lower the amount of fat and increase the amount of fiber, vitamins and complex carbohydrates you eat. Protein powder supplements are not necessary for mountain biking as long as you have a balanced diet. The deliberate administration of amino acids should only be done under medical supervision and should only be done for therapeutic reasons.

Practical Nutrition and Preparation Tips
The daily diet of endurance athletes and of mountain bikers, in particular, should feature at least one portion of pasta, potatoes or rice (whole grain products if possible), to meet the carbohydrate requirements. During the day, a lot of bread (again whole grain or brown bread), with cheese or sweet spreads (thin), should be eaten as light snacks. Various types of muesli without sugar and with porridge oats and fruit is a balanced, healthy meal for any time of day, not just breakfast. For complete sports nutrition, include vegetables and salads as garnish. Local, seasonal products definitely contain more vitamins and minerals than products from abroad or the greenhouse. Fruit can be eaten at any time between meals.

By spreading out the total amount of food consumed in the day into three or four main meals and several snacks, the blood sugar levels and also hunger can be maintained at an even level, thus making controlling your weight easy.

Food preparation should be reduced to a minimum. Long cooking and roasting reduce the amount of vitamins and other nutrients and also the taste of the food. High-quality oils with unsaturated fatty acids and a non-stick frying pan reduce the intake of low-grade fats. Vegetables should only be briefly steamed or eaten raw.

In general, an elite athlete's diet should be sparing but high-quality in order to be able to achieve a small weight loss or to maintain racing weight. During periods of high training intensities and frequent races, this should be abandoned, though. The plain diet is especially important in winter, when training is reduced, to avoid putting on weight.

Calorie counting and combining should be avoided, as they are completely impractical and very time-consuming.

Preparation Phases
At the start of the training year when the total training load is very low, special techniques to increase the glycogen reserves can be abandoned. The nutrition should be adapted to requirements according to the aforementioned criteria. On days with strength training workouts, whether on the bike, at home or in the weight room, the protein intake in the form of meat, fish, dairy products or vegetable proteins (legumes) should be adjusted accordingly.

Racing Phase
In the racing phase, with its very high workloads, pay very special attention to the diet. The following section explores the area of optimal nutrition before, during and after racing. In the training phases during the week, the principles of basic training nutrition should be observed. As the racing phase usually takes place in the summer, pay attention to your fluid consumption, because of the increased loss of fluids during hot weather.

Transition Phase
During the transition phase, the principles of sports nutrition should on no account be ignored, because you may often feel constantly hungry after training camps or intensive training blocks. The body has gotten used to high workloads and equally large amounts of food, and in the first days of reduced training it longs for unlimited amounts of food. Self-discipline, an increased fluid intake and a ban on high-fiber food are required to avoid putting on weight.

7.3   Pre-Race Nutrition

Here are some tips:

- In the days leading up to the race, ensure a high proportion of carbo-hydrates (65%).
- Possibly use carbohydrate loading (see the following).
- The evening before the race, eat an easily digestible, high-carbohydrate, low-fat meal (pasta party).
- Ensure sufficient fluid intake (no alcohol).
- The last, solid, high-carbohydrate meal should be eaten no more than 3–4 hours before the race and must be easy to digest; don't eat too much, but do drink abundantly. No candy.

Fluid Intake

Before a mountain bike race, just like before a long tour, you should make sure you are sufficiently hydrated. A fluid deficit has a very negative impact on performance and can even be dangerous. A simple way of testing the body's fluid levels is by checking the color of your urine. If the urine is dark yellow, as it often is after long training rides with low fluid intake, this is a warning sign that you must drink to avoid starting the race in a dehydrated state. Ideally, urine should be light yellow in color, as this indicates that your fluid levels are balanced. Test your urine so that the evening before the race you give yourself time to top up your water balance with an extra one to two bottles of mineral water, if necessary. Beer should be avoided, as it has a diuretic effect, which is the opposite of what you are trying to achieve.

Pasta Party

Pasta parties, where pasta with a very low-fat sauce is served with abundant drinks, have proven very popular the evening before a race or a big tour. However, you should avoid eating and drinking too much and too late to ensure that your sleep is not disturbed. This high-carb meal is, in many cases, sufficient to fill the glycogen reserves. The carbohydrate loading described next should only be undertaken by elite cyclists.

Race Day

If the race starts in the morning, you will need to get up very early on race day in order to eat a high-carb breakfast or, if necessary, eat pasta again. This should be done three to four hours before the race in order to give the body time to digest. Then drink in small doses until the start and have a few small snacks (e.g., banana chips, muesli bars)) that have as little sugar as possible, and no cola. Sweet snacks, like chocolate bars, temporarily raise blood sugar levels, which then fall at the start of the race and prevent peak performance (see figure 7.1)

For an afternoon start, an early, high-carb lunch should be avoided, as it is the meal the previous evening that is critical for filling the glycogen reserves. An excellent source of carbohydrate is rice pudding, which can also be used to combat hunger between heats and finals, if necessary.

Carbohydrate Loading

Carbohydrate loading just means the deliberate filling of the glycogen reserves before a significant load in order to be able to maintain high speeds for as long as possible.Even with mountain bikers, whose glycogen reserves are already enlarged compared to other athletes due to their high-carb diet, it is possible to top up with a bit more (i.e., loading effect).

Fig. 7.1: Change in blood sugar level with and without carbohydrate intake (e.g. cola, candy) shortly before a 90-minute load.

This is done by following a tough training ride that depletes glycogen reserve with no food intake by reducing training volume and intensity while eating a very high-carbohydrate diet for two to three days. This has the effect of filling the glycogen reserves, especially in the legs, to a greater extent than before (i.e., supercompensation). For a race at the weekend, Wednesday and Thursday are good days for the exhausting workout. The carbohydrate loading begins directly after the tough workout; now is the time to celebrate with your first pasta party!

High glycogen concentrations cause increased water retention in the muscles, which can make the legs feel heavy at the start of the race, but this feeling soon disappears. Carbohydrate loading is only recommended for trained athletes, as no similar supercompensation has been observed in untrained individuals, and large carbohydrate intake could lead to weight gain.

In the carbohydrate loading described below, the exhausting workout is performed on a Thursday, but it can also be done on a Wednesday, prolonging the loading phase by a day. This kind of performance diet is sometimes specialized even further by eating an extremely high-fat and protein diet before embarking on the carbohydrate loading phase described previously. Nutrition and specific diets should not become a punishment, though. Instead, food should taste as it did before. For this reason, carbohydrate loading should be strictly limited to really important races.

Table 7.1: Training and Nutrition Plan for Carbohydrate Loading

Day	Training	Nutrition
Thursday 3	Exhausting training depending on age and ability 2–6 hrs BE 1 with a few tempo sections (RSE), either with the road bike or the MTB, not too much muscular effort	During training: Eat as little as possible; drink a lot. Afterwards: Eat a lot of carbs as soon as possible.
Friday 2	Depending on age and ability, 1–3 hrs BE 1/CT, easy pace, as little muscular effort as possible	High-carb, low-fat food Breakfast: muesli, bread Lunch: pasta, rice, potatoes Dinner: pasta, rice, potatoes
Saturday 1	Depending on age and ability, 1–2 hrs BE 1/CT, easy pace, 1 x 1–4 min BE 2/RSE to test	High-carb, low-fat food Same as Friday, but pasta party in the evening with large portion of carbohydrate (not too late!), drink as much water as possible
Sunday 0	Race	High-carb, easily digestible breakfast, poss. A high-carb lunch, 3–4 hrs before, don't eat too much, no cola

7.4 Nutrition During the Race

It is only necessary to eat during races lasting longer than 60 minutes. If the race lasts longer than 90 minutes, it is essential to consume carbohydrates in order to avoid a drop in performance. In training, depending on your training state, a small carbohydrate snack is only required after about two hours.

Hitting the Wall

In cycling, the state of total exhaustion of the carbohydrate reserves is called bonking, or hitting the wall. Typical symptoms such as hallucinations of food dizziness, loss of concentration, disorientation and significantly reduced performance level, a state that can be very dangerous both on a bike in traffic and off-road on the mountain bike. In order to raise the now very low blood sugar level, it is usually sufficient to eat a few sugar lumps or some glucose. Although this does not significantly improve the performance level, you will quickly feel better and

will then be able to return home or search for food with a clear head. The wall usually affects mountain bikers in the spring in the first longer training rides in still, draining, cold air. With the consumption of high-carbohydrate snacks, especially muesli bars, fruit (e.g., banana, apple, pears, dried fruit), rice cakes, bread (with low-fat spread), cookies and also energy bars, the wall can be prevented and performance levels maintained.

On longer rides, complex carbohydrates are eaten first and the simple sugars (glucose) only near the end of the ride. In order to get an energy boost for the often decisive final spurt, many cyclists drink a little coffee with plenty of sugar about 30 min before the end.

Drinking fluids during the race is extremely important.

Refreshment During a Race (Race Duration: 2 hrs)

Time	Solid foof	Fluids
0:00–0:30 min (start)	You can eat energy or museli after 15 min.	Drink regularly in small sips right from the start.
0:30–1:30 hr (middle)	Eat small bites of energy bars or muesli bars and drink.	Drink energy drinks, isotonic drinks, fruit spritzers regularly.
1:30–2:00 hrs (end)	No more solid food, at most 2–3 tablets of glucose 30 min before the end.	30 min before the end, drink a little (1/2 bottle) cola spread out over several minutes.

Drinking half a bottle of cola or a few tablets of glucose have a similar effect and give an additional performance boost.

Eating on the Bike

Eating on the bike requires practice, as many mountain bike novices often cannot eat while cycling due to stomach problems. The ability to eat while cycling is a detail that is often overlooked. Particularly during longer tours, marathons and the increasingly common MTB stage races, considerable amounts of food must be consumed on the mountain bike, so include this in your training program.

Those who cannot digest solid food must drink fluid carbohydrates, which should be a balanced mixture of simple and complex carbohydrates. An inexpensive way of preparing a high-carbohydrate drink is stirring maltodextrine (found in pharmacies) into water in the drinking bottle. Be careful because this can cause indigestion in high concentrations.

The plan described previously is a simplified presentation of the ideal process. However, it is often impossible over demanding courses to eat and drink regularly; in these cases, just eat and drink when the occasion arises. Important: In races up to two and a half hours long, it is even advisable to consume energy drinks, as described previously, as it is still possible to consume fluids over tricky sections. This is significantly quicker to do and disrupts breathing less.

7.5 Post-Race Nutrition

Post-exercise nutrition plays a key role in recovery. The depletion of glycogen stores increases the activity of the enzyme glycogen synthase, which promotes glycogen formation and storage in the cells. As the concentration of this enzyme is highest between two and four hours after exercise and then reverts to the starting value after 24 hours, the mountain biker must consume sufficient carbohydrate after racing or training to refill his glycogen stores. If this is not done and exercise is resumed the following day, the stores are emptied further. So, glycogen stores are not only emptied by long, intensive exercise, but also by shorter bouts of exercise on consecutive days without refilling the stores in between.

During the first 24 hours after an exhausting race or training ride, there is no difference between the utilization of complex or simple carbohydrates, but after 24 hours, complex carbs significantly increase glycogen synthesis. In addition, complex carbohydrates are more advantageous for health reasons, as they can be absorbed in combination with numerous other nutrients and dietary fiber. After exercise, food like pasta, rice, whole grain products or fruit should be eaten. Immediately after exercise, make use of the two hours that are usually characterized by a lack of appetite for recovery purposes by consuming high-carbohydrate drinks (e.g., not-too-acidic fruit juice, cola). Normally, special energy drinks can be avoided, unless you are taking part in a multiday race or a stage race, where you are pushing yourself to the limit and the recovery time is very short. The fluid loss should be replaced gradually and not all at once. Ice-cold drinks should be avoided due to the increased sensitivity of the gastrointestinal tract. Fruit juices rich in potassium, to enhance glycogen storage, diluted with a good-quality mineral water, restore the fluid balance and also supply minerals and carbohydrates.

7.6 Weight Loss for Bike Racing

Every endurance athlete and mountain biker is familiar with the connection between form and weight; the better your form, the lower your weight. Here we are talking about racing weight, which is different for everyone depending on their constitution and lies between two and eight kilograms below your winter weight.

In general, in winter when training is cut back, the weight should not deviate too much from the racing weight. Often, mountain bikers experience a big performance improvement after losing weight.

How do you drop the pounds?

Long training rides in the fat burning zone, especially in the preparation phase, and a light, reduced calorie diet allow you to burn a few pounds. The diet should be particularly low in fat, but completely meets your protein requirements in order to prevent muscle protein from being metabolized. Also the carbohydrate supply must be adequate to prevent glycogen depletion.

While carbohydrates are digested really quickly and raise blood sugar levels, fats are slow to digest and have a negligible effect on blood sugar levels, so that you feel full for longer. The feeling of rapid satiety obtained from high-carb food therefore facilitates weight loss for all mountain bikers, whatever their level. Long **BE 1** workouts after a very minimal breakfast boost fat burning significantly.

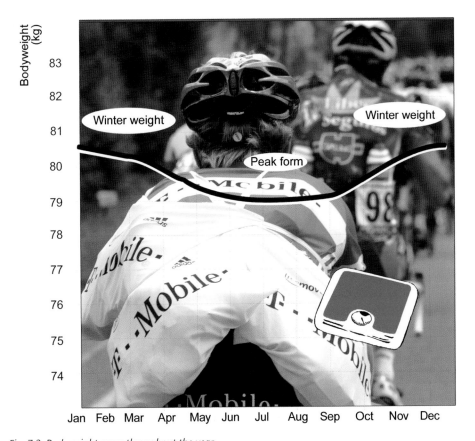

Fig. 7.2: Bodyweight curve throughout the year

Weight reduction tips for elite mountain bikers:
- Extremely low-fat food
- High proportion of carbohydrates, over 60%
- High-carb breakfasts (never go without breakfast)
- High-carb snacks
- Early evening meal, as before sleeping calories make their way to fat depots
- After the evening meal, if possible don't anything else; if you are really hungry, only eat fat-free snacks (e.g., vegetables, fruit)
- Lose weight slowly

You should weigh yourself every morning after going to the bathroom. A balanced energy supply is reflected in a constant bodyweight. Fluctuations in bodyweight between 1–1.5 kilograms, or sometimes up to 2 kilograms, are normal. The important thing is to have a constant average weight.

If an athlete loses too much weight, this can indicate that he is overtraining. Weight loss should be approached with caution, and never exceed a reduction of 1–2 kilograms per month. Figure 7.2 shows the typical weight curve of a mountain biker (cross-country racer) throughout the year.

7.7 Nutrition FAQs

What do you make of energy drinks?
Some mountain bike teams are famously sponsored by energy drink manufacturers. Unfortunately, this suggests that they are suitable for the endurance athlete. These drinks (like cola or coffee) are certainly capable of mobilizing energy reserves if drunk in sufficient quantities, thereby prolonging performance, but they most definitely do not give you wings. They affect different people in very different ways. Ultimately, this is a moral issue, like the problem of doping. Anyone who refuses to boost his performance by doping should also steer clear of these legal methods, because the drop in performance during intensive exercise at the anaerobic threshold actually makes biological sense. It is a protective mechanism. Anyone who ignores these natural limits that can be shifted upward by training too often must deal with undesired side effects.

What are the features of a good energy bar?
There are many kinds of energy bars on the market from many different manufacturers. An energy bar should primarily, thanks to its combination of complex

and simple carbohydrates, enable a short-term and longer-lasting energy supply for the working muscles. Fats and protein should, at most, be present in very low amounts. Additives such as vitamins and minerals, although useful, are not necessary if the diet is balanced. The fat and protein content of many energy bars is too high. This kind of bar is most commonly used by body builders, whose priorities are different to those of endurance athletes.

Key energy bar features should be the taste and edibility, even in colder weather. The bar must be easy to chew, quick to dissolve and easy to swallow in the mouth when you drink at the same time as eating. Energy bars should basically be eaten with a lot of fluid in order to dilute the nutrient concentration already in the stomach and accelerate nutrient absorption. High-fiber energy bars like muesli bars are not useful in races, as firstly they take too long to digest and secondly they contain too little carbohydrate.

Special Nutrition Advice for Women

Due to their physical prerequisites that differ from men's, top female mountain bikers must observe some basic principles where nutrition is concerned to avoid suffering from deficiency symptoms.

As well as the aforementioned sports nutrition factors, women must be sure to consume enough calcium, iron and vitamin B_2.

Missed periods (amenorrhea) in some female endurance athletes (10–20%) is the result of a low estrogen level, which in turn is responsible for osteoporosis. Calcium salts leach out of the bones, reducing bone density. A reduction in estrogen levels can also be observed in female mountain bikers with normal periods, so that calcium-rich foods should be an essential component of any diet. The daily requirement of calcium is 1,200 milligrams, which can easily be covered by dairy products, tofu and fresh vegetables. Meat and lentils are particularly good sources of iron. If consumed at the same time as tea or coffee, iron absorption is reduced by the tannic acid they contain.

The well-known problem of iron deficiency suffered by female athletes also affects mountain bikers, caused by the blood loss during menstruation and a diet that is not appropriate for sport. Symptoms are fatigue and poor performance as well as occasional chills. In many cases, the administration of iron preparationsunder medical supervision is advisable and necessary.

Both male and female bikers can suffer from vitamin B_2 deficiencies, as endurance training diminishes the concentration of vitamin B_2. Vitamin B_2 is used in splitting fats and carbohydrates for energy production and is therefore very important. Good sources of B_2 are dairy products and whole grain products. If you eat a high-quality, balanced diet you do not need to take a B_2 supplement.

8   Technique Training

8.1   The Importance of Technique Training

As already described in chapter 2, coordination and cycling technique make a big contribution to overall cycling performance. Their significance varies from one discipline to another. In the technical disciplines like trial, slalom and downhill, it is extremely important, but less so in cross-country races. Although in comparison to road racing, cross-country races do demand a great deal of technical skill and bike control, the techniques required for cycling in a peloton and in breakaway groups are also complex.

Extreme biking situations must be taken in stride.

In general, cycling technique should be developed as well. As far as training methodology is concerned, in cross-country, marathon and downhill its importance must be weighed against other qualities such as endurance, strength, speed and flexibility, which need a lot of training time to reach the required level, especially endurance and strength. However, good cycling technique can make up for a lack of endurance and strength over demanding cross-country courses, something that can often be observed in older cyclists in the senior age groups. Out of two equally strong mountain bikers, the one with better cycling technique will always prevail.

The professionals seem to be at one with their bikes, and they ride off-road nimbly as a result. But even they, despite apparently having already achieved perfection, must repeatedly train certain techniques and also devote part of their training time to technique work. Any normal cross-country racer who has ridden behind a good downhiller over a steep and awkward single trail, will know just how great the difference in technique can be and what a big time difference this can make at the end of a long descent. The technically demanding sections are often those that are most decisive when it comes to the race result, and it is here, not in the tempo and uphill sections, that many bikers lose crucial seconds and minutes. However, the factor that has most influence on the result of a cross-country race is still endurance.

Safety Through Cycling Technique Training

With the increase in popularity of mountain biking in the 1990s, the number of serious injuries also rose, primarily caused by self-inflicted falls with no outside interference. In the Alps area, the number of seriously injured mountain bikers has overtaken that of motorbike riders. These falls are usually caused by riding downhill too fast—too fast in relation to the nature of the road and the cyclist's own technical proficiency. However, targeted, regular technique training can create a safety net that helps a cyclist in dangerous situations and prevents falls, as long as on dangerous sections he does not constantly try to ride to his own higher limit.

With increasing exhaustion toward the end of the race or training ride, coordination declines considerably, and at times like this, excellent bike control is also a protection against a dangerous fall.

Prerequisites for Good Bike Control

Strong and well-trained arm and leg muscles are important prerequisites for learning and mastering difficult techniques. Furthermore, well-developed core muscles protect against injuries of the passive locomotor system (e.g., bones, ligaments). Your equipment must be in tip-top condition, for technique training causes a lot of wear and tear on it, and occasionally, during technique training or when trying out new moves, defective equipment (e.g. broken fork, chain or handlebars) can be the cause of bad accidents.

Anticipation in Downhills

Good downhillers have the gift of anticipating the course and taking correct actions (i.e., course selection, braking, weight shifting). Anticipation means unconsciously planning ahead to take action that suits the environment. Based on the slightest alterations in terrain or other stimuli, processes in the brain that determine exactly what needs to be done should happen almost automatically. The programmed actions can, however, also still be corrected in the short-term. In most ball games, anticipation plays a key role in order to prepare as early as possible for a shot from your opponent. When downhillers instinctively choose the right racing line, they are showing good anticipation. However, at the same time they must also constantly perceive and process the current situation and adapt their behavior accordingly. These unconscious processes illustrate the complexity of a very technically demanding action and show that good coordination (i.e., quick wit, quick reactions, good anticipation) is absolutely vital in order to deal with difficult sections.

8.2   Choosing the Most Important Cycling Techniques

Coordination as the overall term for cycling technical skills comprises more though than just the different curve, jumping and braking techniques. The pedaling technique must also be perfected in order to optimize cycling economy. The following list features a range of required techniques to be trained. Each technique area can also be subdivided into different individual techniques. Unfortunately, a description of these individual cycling techniques would exceed the scope of this book, although there are a number of books on the market that do cover this subject in more detail.

Balance is the Foundation

The key to a good bike technique is balance. Only those who can hold their body in a standing position on the bike using tiny shifts of bodyweight and the coordination of brakes and pedals will also be able to control their bike during complex technical moves. Consequently, the first priority of a targeted technique training program is learning to stand or jump on the spot with the mountain bike. You should be able to stand in place for a few minutes, just like the sprinters in the velodrome.

Technique area	Individual techniques	Basic skills
Balancing techniques	Trying to stand (resting against the wall or without help) Trying to stand with support from one leg Trying to stand with no hands	Balance
Jumping techniques	Hopping forward Hopping backward Hopping on the back wheel Hopping on the front wheel	Balance Rhythm Strength (speed strength and maximum strength)
Braking techniques	Full brake	Balance Anticipation Feeling of speed
Curve techniques	Laying Pushing Cutting in Drifting Sliding	Balance Anticipation (riding line) Braking
Downhill techniques	Jumps Tempo riding Overcoming steps Balance shifting	Balance Strength Feeling of speed Short reaction times Anticipation (riding line)
Uphill techniques	Riding out of the saddle Sitting Overcoming steps	Balance Load distribution (front, rear wheel) Strength
Acceleration techniques	Acceleration from a standing position Acceleration from a sitting position	Balance Strength
Pedaling techniques	Riding out of the saddle Sitting	Forward phase Backward phase Upward phase Downward phase
Gear-shifting techniques	Shifting up (adapted to terrain) Downshifting (adapted to terrain)	Anticipation

8.3 Technique Training: When and How?

Technique training should be done when the body is in a rested state, as a neuromuscular system that is fatigued after a hard workout will not respond well to coordination work. This means that technique training should either be done in isolation, at the start of a workout, or even as a refresher after an easy ride. In a group workout, the time spent waiting for all participants to gather at the meeting point can be used for technique training. Technique training done in a group is more enjoyable and motivating. It also provides the opportunity to talk and exchange experiences, leading to new insights and a better understanding of some movement sequences. Before technique training, do a a warm-up for a few minutes in the BE 1 zone, followed by a few stretching exercises.

Off-Road With Protective Gear
The training for basic techniques and games is either off-road at selected locations or on a field. A field is advantageous when it comes to the inevitable falls. In-line skating knee and elbow pads are useful for technique training as they are easy to wear and prevent the majority of skin grazes and bruises. Shin pads are also highly recommended, as the shins are very often hurt when jumping. A helmet is another essential for technique training.

Execution
The selected techniques are practiced repeatedly, and you should only move on to another technique after progress has been made on the first. A high number of reps must be performed before complex movement sequences are mastered. Ideally, technique training and mental training should be combined (see chapter 9). The best results are obtained by alternating the two training methods as described.

You still need cycling technique reserves when riding at your limit.

A short circuit of just a few hundred yards in the forest or an old gravel pit can be set up using tree trunks and other objects so that it is very technically demanding. Frequently riding round this circuit in both directions is a fun way to improve your bike control. A technique training workout lasts about 30–60 minutes. In longer workouts, the motor learning ability declines sharply. Technique training should be carried out at least once a week for cross-country and marathon riders. However, repeated, short exercises of a few minutes (e.g., when waiting for your training partner after a few tricky sections) are very effective and sometimes achieve more than a long technique workout.

Start young

The earlier you start technique training, the easier it is to learn difficult movement sequences. Adults usually need a lot more time to learn a technique and also a lot of patience. Children and youth practice, fall and practice again. For adults, falls and the associated injuries represent a major obstacle in technique training. After a few bad experiences, many bikers give up and settle for a merely average technical level.

8.4   Exercise Circuit

If you train with a group, it is fun to build an exercise circuit. This circuit can be made of natural and man-made obstacles. A kind of coordination or skills competition motivates and is especially fun for kids. Another way of putting the learned techniques into practice is doing training races round a very technical, short circuit. Here you can take lap time-trials or pursuit races like in the velodrome. Every mistake is given a time penalty (e.g., 5 sec) or penalty points.

The **road** bike exercise circuit is easy to build and provides all abilities with a great challenge when learning better bike control.

Ideas for an exercise circuit:

1. See-saw

A board is laid across a tree trunk or a beam. As you ride over it, the board tips to the other side. Whoever doesn't make the see-saw has an error.

2. Ski jumps

With a board and a beam, build a small ramp. A good "kicker" can be made out of clay, although this does require a bit of digging. Whoever does not dare to jump gets a time penalty or a penalty point.

3. Rope as a high obstacle

A taught rope or barrier tape forces the biker to jump and rebound to train the bike-run transition. Only if the technique is very clean and without rope contact are no time penalties or other penalties awarded.

4. Tree trunk

Fixed tree trunks or beams of varying diameter must be crossed or jumped over with the bike, without dismounting. Ground contact is an error.

5. Slalom or trial course

With stones, branches, barrier tape and cones, build a slalom course. Touching the ground with the feet is an error.

6. Bumps/tree roots

Rough stretches with bumps or tree roots make good connecting sections and are good places to practice compensating for impact and balance.

7. Dip/hole/hill

For practicing steep downhills and steep climbs. The initial gradient must be very steep, enabling you to drop into the short downhill or conquer a climb in which your feet must not touch the ground.

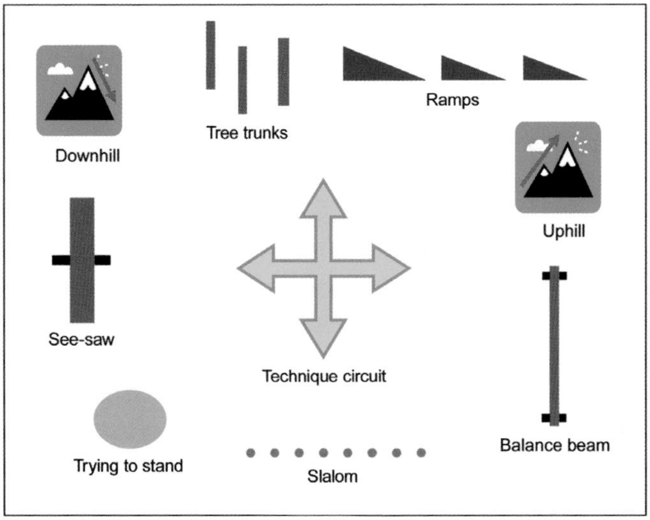

8. Balance beam

Riding along a beam or a line trains balance. You can also ride along dry tree trunks. If you fall, you get a time penalty.

Fig. 8.1: Example exercise circuit

All kinds of jumps must be mastered.

Skills decathlon:

1. Trying to stand (every 10 sec = 1 point)

2. Wheelie (every 5 sec = 1 point)

3. Limbo ride under a stretched elastic line. The elastic is 6 in higher than the highest part of each rider's bike (3 points for going under).

4. Pick-up small objects from the ground (e.g., leaves, sticks, coins) (1 point per object).

5. Balancing Ride down a narrow, 2.5–5-inch wide and 2-m long beam (2 points if successful).

6. Throw a ball into a goal (bin) while riding the bike. Ideally, throw from a few yards away so that the speed is similar for all participants (3 attempts, 1 point per goal).

7. Drawing a figure with a piece of chalk (e.g., a large circle or a house on the ground). For each new stroke start again. (2 points if successful).

8. Slalom course timed (set a minimum time, 3 points if successful, take off 1 point for every pole or cone knocked over).

9. Tire slashing Like a knight on a steed, try to put a stick through hanging rings (1 point per ring) when riding on the bike. A slightly swinging ring is a real challenge.

10. Can hitting at high speed; a tin can is placed on a branch or other object that must be knocked off (3 attempts, 1 point for each successful attempt).

8.5 Small Games and Exercises With the Mountain Bike

Small games with the mountain bike are great fun and enable an anxiety-free, un-conscious learning of bike control even with body and bike contact. If necessary, wear the protective gear described previously. A smooth, flat field is the ideal location.

Games:

1. Soccer
Soccer on mountain bikes is great fun and works quite well after a while. Goalkee-pers are not needed as the goals are only 1-m wide. The game should basically be played with no physical contact between the opponents.
Caution: The front chain rings can cause injuries to the legs.
Variation: The bikes are used as scooters, with one free leg to push off from the ground.

2. Basketball
Basketball can also be played on mountain bikes. However, the ball can't be dribbled forward, just carried as you ride along.
Variation: When shooting at the hoop, no ground contact with the feet.

3. Relay games
All kinds of relays are excellently suited to MTB games. On the courses, obstacles can be set up for added difficulty. Small tasks can also be completed along the course. For example, set up two slalom courses that must be ridden simultaneously by two teams (dual slalom). However, relay games are advanced games in which the tempo should be kept low by the choice of course and obstacles. Relay games are not suitable for beginners.

4. Show jumping
A number of different obstacles are set up that form a course that must be jumped or ridden over. One error point is awarded for each failed obstacle. The winner is the one who makes the least mistakes and has the fastest time. Other obstacles or tasks can also be included.

5. Tag
Many games of tag can also be played on mountain bikes. They are fast, intense and great fun. Rules (e.g., only the lowest gear) and a reduction in the size of the playing field should be imposed to keep the speed down.

6. Master and hound

In the braking game master and hound, the hound must brake at the master's command, "Sit" and must not under any circumstances stop in front of the master's front wheel. After braking, stay in the balance position for a few seconds and only then ride on. The hound follows the master with his front wheel level with his master's rear wheel. The master gradually increases the speed, brakes immediately after the sudden command and tries to outwit the hound.

7. Run-bike

Two cyclists form a team with just one bike between them. One of them runs while the other cycles. If the runner is exhausted, they swap over. Run-bike is an exciting and very demanding team race, which is all about the optimal interaction between the partners. Differences in ability can be balanced out by using different course lengths.

8. MTB biathlon

On a technically demanding circuit, four to six bikers start simultaneously. Each time they finish a lap, there is a "shooting" in which the bikers must throw objects (e.g., fir cones) into a bin or circle on the ground (e.g., allow only four throws). For each mistake, a penalty lap or push-ups must be performed.

9. Eliminator

The eliminator is a qualifying ride that culminates in a final. On a demanding circuit, two to six cyclists ride against each other. The best two go on to the next round (heats–semi-final–final). For all the others, repêchages can be held, if required.

10. Trying to stand

In a marked field, the bikers must stand in place or ride slowly. The referee makes the field smaller, and whoever touches the ground must leave the field and practice standing further. The last one to remain inside the field is the winner.

Pushing out variants: 1) The bikers must push each other away with hands on the handlebar, and **2)** the bikers must push each other out with one hand. Anyone who is out has to do a timed, technically demanding circuit after which he is allowed back in the game.

11. Bike swap

Two bikers swap bikes when standing and then ride away from each other, with the bikes close together. One brake must always be applied on each bike. They may not tread on spokes, gears or disk brakes. The change is easiest to do if one partner changes over the back wheel.

12. Crossing
Biker A and biker B stand next to each other in one direction. They are not allowed to turn around. Start on a signal. The bikers try to cross behind each other (the bikes must always remain facing the direction of travel).

13. Bike duathlon
Every participant must complete a running course, then perform one or more laps on the bike and then finally do another run (duration of the exercise is variable).

14. One too many
Just like the game musical chairs, the idea is to occupy a certain place with the bikes. Suitable objects are a beer coaster, stick or stone. There must always be one less place available than the number of participants in the group.

15. Tail catching
The traditional running game also works on bikes, with a piece of barrier tape that is 1.5-feet long. The playing field should be as small as possible to keep the speed down. The gear ratio can also be fixed (low gears = low speed).

Technique training with the bike-parcours

16. Six-minute race

Just like the six-day race, teams of two race against each other. At any one time, one team member is racing and the other just pedals slowly or rests. The bikers not in the race ride around on a very short, open circuit (oval) while they wait in a takeover zone in the finish area to join the race that takes place on a longer off-road trail (see also exercise 5, hand sling maneuver).

17. Slow mountain

Two or three cyclists ride as slowly as possible along an uphill trail (10–50 m) that is appropriate for their abilities. By riding slowly, the leading rider tries to force the back marker to quit by touching the ground with his foot, for example, at which point the riding order changes. If both or all riders reach the top with no mistakes, they get one point. The first to get three points wins.

Exercises:

1. Pushing away

In order to practice coping with physical contact during races, while riding slowly side by side in pairs with your upper bodies leaning against each other (i.e., in an inclined position), try to push each other away.

2. Touching rear wheels

Two bikers ride one in front of the other, trying to alternately touch the rear wheel of their partner with their own front wheel without falling off. See if you can touch your partner's rear wheel 3 times in a row while riding under control.
Variation: Touch the front of the rear wheel.

3. Scooter

The bike is used as a scooter. This gives a whole new feeling to curves and slaloms. Even shadow riding one behind the other is fun to do like this.

4. Formation riding

Grasp the stem of the bike next to you to form a long chain. Can a group of 10 ride a curve? Can the group stop? Start in pairs and then slowly increase the numbers.

5. Hand sling maneuver

The hand sling is normally used in the velodrome in two-man team racing. Mountain bikers can also use it to practice their bike control. One cyclist rides slowly and places his left hand palm-down on his bottom. The faster cyclist rides up behind him, grips the open hand with his right hand and transfers his speed to the slower rider, by catapulting him forward. Increase speed slowly!

6. Riding blind
One partner is blindfolded and the other leads him on foot over safe terrain, ideally keeping a hand on the blindfolded rider's back at all times (do not hold the handlebar). Later on he can walk beside the blindfolded rider with no physical contact, just guiding him with acoustic signals.

7. S-slides
Block the rear wheel brake, take your bodyweight off the rear wheel by shifting your weight forward and slowly move the handlebar to describe one or more letter Ss on an unmade road.

8. Slow climbs
Experts can try to ride steep climbs very slowly but without losing balance and needing to touch the ground with their feet.

9. Acrobatics on the bike
Bikers use their creativity to try to adopt figures and positions on their moving bikes, inspired by trick cycling moves. Also explore how two people can ride on the bike at the same time.

10. Holding hands
Two bikers ride side-by-side, holding hands at varying tempos and round curves. This can also be done by a cross-over grip on the partner's bike stem.

11. Stubborn donkey
One partner grips his brakes harder and harder, pretending to be a stubborn donkey that his partner attempts to pull along.

12. Standing at an obstacle
With the front wheel resting against a wall or a tree, try to stand up.

13. Jump and turn
Jumping in place, try to complete a turn. Who can get round the furthest?

14. Bike shifting
Try to move forward by alternately hopping on the front and rear wheel.

15. Tight turn
On a narrow lane, try to turn without touching the ground. A narrow path can also be marked out with ropes, sticks or cones.

16. Special slalom
A cone slalom course is not normally done with the front wheel, but this time try to ride around the cones, passing them with the part of the bike between the front wheel and the frame (down tube). The higher the cones, the harder the exercise.

17. Tin can shooting
Empty drinks cans or plastic bottles should be shot away by lifting the front wheel briefly and whipping the handlebar round to hit them.

18. Figure braking
With a blocked rear wheel, create symbols and figures on the ground. Who is the most creative? Who can draw a symbol most quickly?

19. Star kiss

Two to six bikers approach a marking in star formation and touch each other above the marking with their front wheels. They then try to pull the bike back and ride away without touching the ground. Backward hopping is also allowed.

All of the above games and exercises from the multi-event contest can be combined at will with another circuit or a new multi-event contest. With a little creativity, rules can be altered and new variations or even completely new games invented. The games are most enjoyable in groups of six or more cyclists.

9   Psychological Training

Anyone who has ever sat on a mountain bike knows only too well in which kind of situations he feels mentally blocked. A steep step, a descent, a jump or a steep climb can trigger fear. Fear of not being able to cope with the passage, but above all, a fear of falling.

Psychological training enables you to do a lot more than just overcome fear, as it can also produce outstanding results in the areas of coordination and technique training. Furthermore, mental preparation for a race is vital for maximizing motivation. But a great deal of motivation is also required for training, and mental training can help you achieve this too. The various relaxation techniques are also very useful to promote recovery.

9.1   When Fear Gets in the Way

Fear as a form of mental tension is very often the psychological escape route from a threatening situation, which could occur or already has occurred (e.g., a fall). It is the reflection of the subconscious. As well as the specific fear of falling and its consequences, in mountain biking there are also more complex fears, such as the fear of defeat, victory or humiliation. Even the presence of other competitors can trigger feelings of fear.

In extreme sections like this, fear must be channeled.

If you want to do something about your fear, it is important to recognize anxiety triggers and be able to put them into words, for this is sometimes all it takes to get your fear under control. Talking to someone you trust or your coach can help to pin down these factors.

Many bikers are always afraid in certain situations in which they regularly feel blocked and which prevent them from achieving their potential. This fear can be expressed in many different ways and have different causes.

How is the fear expressed?

As an outsider, it is difficult to diagnose fear in or before certain situations, for triggers are individual experiences; a few external symptoms can, however, provide information about the fear:

Physical symptoms: shaking, stomach problems, pallor, accelerated pulse
Motor symptoms: poor coordination, cramps, mistakes
Behavior: abnormal behavior, such as excessive aggression or passivity

How can fear be conquered?

This book is limited to a brief presentation of the self-regulatory methods that can be done by you. This fear-reduction training should be done several times a week and, particularly, just before a race (especially downhill).

Physical Procedure

Firstly, fear as a state of psychological arousal can be reduced by physical activity, such as a thorough warm-up. Secondly, the relaxation techniques described next are usually really helpful when it comes to controlling fear, as relaxation is the foundation of fear management.

Mental Process

In the mental process, the fear-triggering negative thoughts must be reevaluated or reinterpreted by trying to think realistically and positively. Reevaluating and putting the importance of a race into perspective reduces the pressure considerably and allows you to take part in the race in a more relaxed state.

As for the very common fear of falling, the greatest success is usually achieved by visualizing correct, completely safe and harmonious techniques like drifting, jumping or the absorbing of hard shocks. However, there is the danger that this visualization may lead to an increased willingness to take risks. Especially where the downhill is concerned, it is important that the visualized techniques are realistic. Incorrect or unrealistic techniques or falls must be totally eliminated from the mind and visualization program (think positive).

9.2 Build Motivation Using Realistic Goals

Look for Mid-Level Races

To promote the development of mental performance ability, look for races that are neither too easy nor too hard but are appropriate for your physical and psychological form. A very easy race against weak opposition would make you overestimate your physical and psychological performance levels, while an overly difficult race would have the opposite effect.

Set Realistic Goals

Just as much care should be taken when setting goals to train toward as when selecting races. If the goal is many years away (e.g., winning a world championship title) and is also unrealistic, you will soon lose sight of it and be aimless again. If a goal is insufficiently challenging, motivation will remain low, as will the amount of effort you put into your training and racing (see chapter 6).

Switching Off From Mountain Biking

To be able to relax mentally and retain your motivation for training and racing, you need to be able to switch off from mountain biking when you get off your bike. Athletes who think about cycling the whole year day-in, day-out usually have mental blocks and put themselves under too much pressure.

Mental Approach

Your mental approach has a direct influence on your physical, mental, technical and tactical performance levels and motivation. Winners are characterized by a great self-confidence, which losers often lack. Your first victory, your first podium or your first marathon are decisive stages on the way to gaining confidence in your own sporting ability.

Winning is in the Head

The mind of a biker must be ready for peak performance, for winning starts in the head and not in the legs.

Warming up as part of a race preparation program provides psychological security.

You will not be mentally capable of either giving your all or being successful until you are able to cope easily with the loading situation. An optimal mental approach is the only way for athletes to achieve results which they do not seem physically capable. In such success situations, one such mental state is *in flow* (i.e., mind and body are in harmony). Racing cyclists often describe this in flow state retrospectively, saying that they were no longer consciously aware of the extreme loads (pain) of a race situation (successful breakaway attempts) or a tour, but just rode relatively loosely and relaxed at a pace that they had never been able to manage before. While people are normally only able to exhaust a certain percentage of their absolute performance capacity, in certain mental states, it is easier for them to tap these performance reserves. It is mental training that allows the gap between real and absolute performance capacity to be reduced.

Motivation

Motivation is highly influenced by how you evaluate your own performance, and it is often a good idea in mental training to start by reevaluating your own performance, as success is hindered by under- or overestimation. A change in evaluation is very easy to achieve in conversation with a trusted adult (e.g., coach, parent or friend). Mental training is now used to try to discover and implement hidden motivation reserves. Simple methods of increasing motivation are things like changing the training environment (training camp), having a break from training (a few days) or practicing other sports in winter. You should also give yourself small rewards for achieving goals.

9.3   Mental Technique Training

As already mentioned, visualization helps you to improve tricky cycling techniques on the bike. When you imagine all the detail involved in a technique, your brain sends impulses to the muscles involved in the movement, just as it would in the actual movement itself. These very weak impulses are not externally visible, but may be felt as twitches. These impulses also show in an electromyogram (electrical impulse of muscles). In this way, specific movement patterns can already be stored and initiated. This form of mental training is particularly important for downhillers and trial riders, who prior to a race can often be spotted in a secluded place going through the race mentally in advance. Mentally withdrawn athletes can often be observed prior to the competition in sports such as ski racing, bobsleigh and high-diving.

Think in Images

Visualization involves freeing oneself from words and thinking in images, which can be further supported by imagined noises, smells and feelings, so that you allow a movement or action to run before your mind's eye like a film.

It is also possible, to visualize riding an optimal race or different emotional target states (e.g., poise, motivation) and likewise, tactical situations after a little practice.

It is important to start with simple movements and only attempt more difficult situations after the simple movements have successfully implemented. Newcomers to mental training should practice for a few minutes as often as possible, ideally every day.

Visualization is not always successful for every athlete straight away, and many bikers never really take to it.

The visualization technique can be carried out almost anywhere and can be especially useful during required training breaks due to injury.

This is how it's done:

1. Before starting to visualize, write down in detail the techniques or tactics you want to improve.

2. The next step is to read through what you have written several times during the next few days and try to see the situation in your mind's eye, changing the text if necessary.

3. When you know the text almost by heart, start to imagine the situation with your eyes closed, maybe even imagining verbal encouragement. It may be helpful to record the text and then play it back and listen to it while you visualize. Furthermore, the tricky part of the movement should be marked and described verbally in a few words (e.g., push, up, round, hop).

4. The last step is then the visualizing the movement, during which you can either feature as the actor like in a film (i.e., watching as an observer) or—better yet—see the situation through your own eyes. After a little while, try to let the visualization run in real time (i.e., jump in your mind from key movement to key movement).

The actions should take place in the present, never in the past, and always correspond to reality. Incorrect movements or actions should be avoided when visualizing because they are then memorized as a kinetic image. Over time, as your experience in dealing with visualization grows, you will develop your own techniques and methods that best suit your own needs.

5. Only when the short film runs quickly and corresponds to real time (about one week) should you proceed to the implementation of the movement with the aid of visualization. In technique training, the visualization technique should be alternated with attempts at the actual movement. For example, start by visualizing riding a wheelie twice, then make five to eight practical attempts.

Before the Race
In the training phase, it is useful to train mentally as well as physically, by visualizing technical, tactical and mental skills. On the day before, or directly before, a race, visualize the specific tactics and mental readiness for the race.

During the Race
On the bike, it is even possible to recall an imaginary program that renders the preceding relaxation phase unnecessary. Short tactical instructions (e.g., riding in front, following a specific cyclist), technical movements (e.g., drifting into the curve or only braking very late) as well as motivational instructions (e.g., keep on going, give your all, ride loose and easy, pedal smoothly) can quickly be remembered and implemented with the aid of the previously trained images.

Imagine a Motivating Image
Mountain biking, like other endurance sports, always involves a struggle between mind and body at some point during the intense effort. In such situations when you are close to giving up, it is useful to have an image that helps the mind to win the struggle and seems to make the task easier than it actually is. The choice of image (e.g., an imaginary picture of a beach, a sunny meadow of flowers, a rope that is pulling you toward the finish line) is up to you. Also the image of something nice, a kind of post-effort reward, can often work miracles and make it easier to dig deep and mobilize your last reserves.

After the Race
After racing or training, start by identifying your mistakes and then visualizing the correct actions, but never the mistakes. Always imagine yourself performing the movements playfully and easily.

9.4 Mental Race Preparation: Optimal Excitement

It is essential to be in an optimal state of arousal to be able to compete to the best of your ability. If you are over-excited or almost apathetic, your performance during the race will be hindered by a mental block.

The aim of mental training must, therefore, be the creation of an optimal state of arousal. Usually mountain bikers tend to be too nervous before a race; it is rare for them to be insufficiently aroused and feeling apathetic and indifferent.

Over-excitement can be managed by relaxation techniques and apathy can be combatted by motivational techniques.

9.4.1 Relaxation Techniques

Relaxation techniques should always be used when you are in a state of emotional tension. Tension caused by anxiety, stress, pressure to succeed or insecurity is called *negative tension*, while tension caused by joy, motivation or self-confidence is referred to as *positive tension*. Before a race, it is necessary to eliminate the negative tension by means of a relaxation technique, thereby creating an optimal state of arousal. Equally, excessive positive tension can be controlled by a relaxation technique. It is up to the individual to determine their own optimal arousal level.

Progressive Muscle Relaxation
Progressive muscle relaxation is a relaxation method first developed by G. Jacobsen in 1934, which is highly suitable for sports because it is easy to learn and works well. It involves the isometric contraction (i.e., contraction without moving the joints) of individual muscle groups followed by the progressive relaxation of the muscles, which has a psychological effect.
It is best to practice for about 10 minutes each day (e.g., before going to bed, or in bed if you have trouble going to sleep). Before a race, leave at least 30 minutes between the relaxation phase and the start, as otherwise you would be too relaxed. A shortened program can be used to get in the mood for visualization.
Progressive muscular relaxation can be carried out either sitting or lying down, although it is more comfortable and more effective lying down. To start with, it is easier to work with a partner who gives you the relaxation instructions in a calm voice. The techniques to be used with each muscle group are as follows:

1. Concentration on the group of muscles or the part of the body.
2. Maximum contraction of the muscle in question, holding for 8–10 seconds.
3. On a signal, relax for about 30 seconds and concentrate on the area concerned.

Mountain bikers should start by relaxing the leg muscles, which can be done at the end, if necessary.

This is what the sequence looks like:
1. Left thigh
2. Left lower leg
3. Left foot
4. Right thigh
5. Right lower leg
6. Right foot
7. Abs
8. Back
9. Left upper arm
10. Left hand and forearm
11. Right upper arm
12. Right hand and forearm
13. Front and back of the neck
14. Face

If speed is of the essence, both sides of the body can be done at the same time. Variations to the program, such as dealing with the individual muscles, especially in the legs, in a more differentiated way, are possible at any time.

Breathing Exercise
Deliberate breathing is also a quick way of relaxing. This involves exhaling very deliberately for a few minutes. The breathing exercises should first be practiced calmly when lying down. Later on, relaxation can be induced even in hectic situations just by prolonged exhalation. A moan or sigh has a similar but involuntary effect.

Autogenic Training
Autogenic training is a form of mental training that should only be learned under the supervision of an experienced expert and requires a great deal of practice compared to the other techniques presented here.

Unfortunately, sports psychology methods have only been given a brief introduction in this book, although there are many books on the market that explore this topic in greater detail. It is important to have an open attitude to mental training, the courage to try something new and a little perseverance.

9.4.2 Marshalling your Resources

The best way to marshal your resources if you are feeling apathetic is by physical activity. A strict pre-race preparation program is particularly important for bikers who are prone to indifference and yawn before a race. Idly hanging around should be avoided, as it just increases the feeling of apathy. A thorough warm-up, inspection of the course and a stretching program will help to marshal your mental resources.

Basically, a strict, unchanging pre-race preparation program is advisable for all mountain bikers, as this little ritual gives a feeling of security. A program could go like this: prepare bike, fetch number, course inspection, mental training (relaxation), warm-up, stretching, put on racing clothes, number, final equipment check, final mental preparation, start.

Unplanned events should not unsettle an athlete, but should be accepted with humor.

9.5 The Right Mental Approach to Training

Different psychological techniques can also be used to prepare for training. This is particularly important for intensive workouts such as hard intervals in which a lot of willpower is needed. The day before or directly before training, imagine, in a short mental movie, the optimal execution of the training session with all the planned content (intervals). This often helps you to keep going in the final sprints or last minutes or seconds of an interval. A poor mental approach often means an unfinished workout.

However, mental training is not helpful if the fundamental will to train and achieve is lacking. The original motivation must come from deep inside you.

Exhaustion after the race: The race result and self-confidence affect future training motivation.

9.6   Recovery Through Relaxation

The various relaxation techniques also aid recovery, as you need to recover mentally as well as physically from exercise. In addition, the contraction–relaxation sequence of the progressive muscle relaxation method significantly reduces muscle tone, which definitely boosts physiological recovery. Other relaxation techniques have a similar effect.

9.7   Mental Pre-Race Program

Performed the evening before or on race day, the following process can help you prepare mentally for the upcoming performance. Allow at least 30 minutes between the end of the mental preparation and the start of the race. Look for a comfortable place in which you can be undisturbed for about 20 minutes and sit or, better still, lie down with your legs relaxed next to each other without touching as your feet fall gently outward.

1. Progressive muscle relaxation
With your eyes closed, first relax physically with your own or the muscle relaxation program described previously, paying particular attention to your legs.

2. Positive thoughts
Now try to move mentally to a pleasant location that gives you a feeling of calm, safety and relaxation; it can be a field, a beach, the forest or similar. The mind should only be in this place and should concentrate on these positive thoughts.

3. Visualization
Once you have successfully completed the first two steps of physical and mental relaxation, the next step is the visualization of the upcoming race or tour itself. This involves imagining yourself on the course and simulating positive, winning tactics and technique. Anticipated difficulties (e.g., uphills and downhills) are overcome with playful ease. Try to create a positive, performance-enhancing attitude to the upcoming effort; the race should be enjoyable. You may also visualize a positive race result.

4. Snapping out of it
Once your visualization session has ended with you winning the race, snap out of your state of relaxation by stretching energetically. On race day you should now focus on the warm-up. The evening before a race, you don't need such a rude awakening, especially if you are then going to sleep.

10

10 Mountain Bike Racing for Beginners

Anyone who has only recently discovered mountain biking knows how hard it is to obtain the right information at the right time. Usually, as in other sports, newcomers must learn the hard way, for the racing scene can seem impenetrable to an outsider.

The next section contains a few tips and tricks that have been assembled to provide comprehensive information, saving you time and stress.

With a few hundred miles under their belts and a relatively secure cycling technique, most bikers start to think about entering races. Compared to road racing, where keep-fit riders are the exception, mountain biking has a very active beginners scene. Irrespective of which discipline you go for (cross-country, downhill, dual slalom, trial, marathon), most race events hold suitable races for many age groups.

The preparations required on the road to the starting line of your first race are described in detail in the next section, and the overview diagram makes it simple for every ambitious beginner.

Making Your First Contact With the Bike Dealer
The bike store is the right place to start for those wanting to take up the sport, as it is the best place to find the information you need. Bike shops also often organize tours and training rides, or the mountain bikers from the nearest club meet there before training. First make sure that the store actually sells mountain bikes or racing bikes. In big cities, this may not always be the case.

Gathering Information From Magazines
Detailed information about the racing scene can be found in the various monthly mountain bike magazines. You will find race calendars and race addresses, updates about equipment and clothing as well as race reports.

The race calendar in the mountain bike magazines and the accompanying address list will definitely help you find an open race nearby that you can enter without having a license.

Entering Races
You usually have to enter races in advance, and this is generally taken care of by the club race manager. However, it is possible to enter some open races yourself

for a small entry fee. The sometimes pricy entry fees may at first seem shocking, but they are justified by the amount of organization that goes into putting on a race. It is better to enter a race in writing (email, fax or postcard). Make sure you respect the closing date, which is usually one to two weeks before the race date. You will usually have to pay a higher fee if you enter after this date.

If you have no desire to enter races, think about entering mountain bike tours, which are well-organized and without race pressure. Mountain bike marathons, although they may often be ridden competitively, do offer the opportunity of participating in a big mountain biking event without putting yourself under pressure to race. However, remember that you do need a good state of fitness to enter long races.

License Races

If you want to start contesting license races immediately, which is only recommended for young beginners, ask your bike dealer for the addresses of local clubs. Another way of obtaining club addresses is by contacting the local, city or state sports association, who will be glad to give you the information you need.

	Children 10-14	Youth 15-16	Boys 17-18	Girls 17-18	Men 19-40	Women 19-40	Seniors Men 41+	Seniors Women 41+
Cross-country	X	X	X	X	X	X	X	X
Downhill			X		X	X	X	
4-Cross			X		X		X	
Trial		X	X		X		X	
Marathon			X	X	X	X	X	X
Cross-country distances	up to 20 min depending on age	30-45 min	45-60 min	45-60 min	60-105 min	60-105 min	45-75 min	45-75 min
Distance profile	Challanging; oftentimes easier course layout in youth races							
Max. entry feer	3€	3€	8€	8€	15€	15€	15€	15€
Numbers of participants	10-20	10-20	10-20	1-5	50-100	5-20	10-40	1-5
Frequency of events	++	+	+	-	++	0	+	-

Fig. 10.1: License races: Classification and information about different race types (Germany)

To be able to enter a license race, you must possess a valid license, which you can only obtain through a club. Choose a club that is based as near as possible to where you live so you can take part in the training activities. There are now many clubs purely for mountain bikers. Often, cycling clubs have mountain biking sections, which have the advantage of having a choice of training groups and partners for the more boring basic or road training sessions.

The First Race

If you have decided to enter a race, you should plan your training accordingly (see chapter 3 for how this works). On the day before the race, check over your equipment. Brakes and gears should be working smoothly.

On race day morning, have a high-carb breakfast, prepare your drinking bottles and race refreshments (also for before and after the race) and pack your bags.

It's a good idea to make a list the day before, as otherwise you will probably forget an important item. When you have more racing experience under your belt, you will be able to pack your bags without thinking.

When you arrive at the race venue, first put your bike together, get your race number or register if necessary and inspect the course. The course inspection is really important for mountain bikers, and you must always allow plenty of time for it. Arrive at the race venue about two to three hours before the start so that you can prepare for the race without rushing and not be thrown by unexpected events. Then put on your racing gear and warm up thoroughly. Your pre-race procedure should become a ritual which also gives you the necessary feeling of mental security (see chapter 9).

By sticking to these golden rules, your first race will almost certainly be a success. However, don't expect too much in terms of result, as you should be pleased just to finish the race without falling or injuring yourself. A lot of time and experience is required in a demanding and training-intensive sport like mountain biking before you can achieve peak performance.

Bibliography

Appel, H.-J. & Stang-Voss, C. (1991): *Funktionelle Anatomie*. Berlin

Baumann, S. (1998): *Psychologie im Sport.* Aachen

Bohlmann, J. T. (1981): Injuries in competetive cycling. *The Physician and Sportsmedicine*

Burke, E. R. (2003): *High-Tech Cycling*. Champaign

Edwards, S. (2001): *Leitfaden zur Trainingskontrolle*. Aachen

Eberspächer, H. (2007): *Mentales Training*. München

Ericson, M. et al. (1986): Power Output and Work in Different Muscle Groups during Ergometer Cycling. In: *Eur. J. appl. Physiol. 55*, 229-235

Harre, D. (1985): *Trainingslehre*. Berlin

Jacobsen, G. (1938): *Progressive Relaxation*. Chicago

Marées, de H. (2008): *Sportphysiologie*. Köln

Markworth, P. (1986): *Sportmedizin*. Hamburg

Matheny, F. (1988): *Beginning bicycle racing*. Brattleboro

Neumann, G., Pfützner, A. & Berbalk, A. (2010): *Optimales Ausdauertraining*. Aachen

Neumann, G. & Berbalk, A. (1991): Umstellung und Anpassung des Organismus – grundlegende Voraussetzungen der sportlichen Leistungsfähigkeit. *Bernett & Jeschke (Hrsg.): Sport und Medizin. Pro und Contra. W. Zuckschwerdt*, München

Pickel, H. & Pecher, S.: Fallstudien. *BikeSportNews 6/97*

Radcliffe, J.C. (1999): *Sprungkrafttraining*. Aachen

Schmidt, A. (2010): *Handbuch für Radsport*. Aachen

Schmidt, A. (*1993)*: Stretching für Radfahrer. *Radfahren extra 2* . Bielefeld.

Tobias, M. & Sullivan, J. (1992): *The complete stretching book*. London

Ungerleider, S. (1996): *Mental training for peak performance*. Emmaus

Zintl, F. (1990): *Ausdauertraining*. München

Photo Credits

Cover photo:	Team Multivan Merida / picture bottom left: Scott
A. Schmidt:	52, 65, 98, 105, 116, 152, 153, 149, 152, 181, 184, 204, 208, 219, 222, 227, 230, 244
Bergamont:	135
Humpert:	47
H. Roth:	56, 58, 90, 102, 114, 115, 138, 206, 211
Team Multivan Merida:	3, 14, 35, 38, 40, 44, 47, 49, 51, 53, 59, 66, 123, 127, 144, 155, 158, 159, 167, 168, 169, 170, 171, 172, 175, 190, 197, 208, 213, 216, 224, 234, 238, 241, 246, 248, back cover photo
Scott:	3, 8, 12, 13, 16, 43, 44, 49, 50, 100, 103, 121, 126, 129, 132, 135, 161, 162, 166, 176, 178, 194, 199, 209, 210, 214, 215, 216, 217, 218, 221, 231,232, 233, 243, 251
Sigmasport:	83, 249
FLEET skates:	105
SRM:	138, 143
Swisspower MTB-Team/ Scott:	106, 109
VDO-Cyclecomputing:	82
www.felt.de/pd-f:	11
Withings:	193
Cover design:	Sabine Groten
Type setting:	Andreas Reuel

CYCLING AND MORE

Mark Kleanthous

THE COMPLETE BOOK OF TRIATHLON TRAINING

The Encyclopedia of Triathlon

This book is for all athletes who want to improve in or convert to the fascinating sport of triathlon. It shows among other things how to construct a training program, how to approach a competition and offers an encyclopedia that covers all aspects of triathlon.

2nd revised edition

376 p., in color,

111 photos, 57 illus.,

Paperback, 6 ½ x 9 ¼

ISBN: 9781782550228

$24.95 US/$ 29.95 AUS

£16.95 UK/€19.95

MEYER & MEYER Sport
Von-Coels-Str. 390
52080 Aachen
Germany

Phone   +49 02 41 - 9 58 10 - 13
Fax   +49 02 41 - 9 58 10 - 10
E-Mail   info@m-m-sports.com
E-Books   www.m-m-sports.com

All books available as E-books.

MEYER & MEYER SPORT